MORE TITLES BY KATHI PELTON

30 Days to Breakthrough: Stepping into Peace

The Yielding: A Lifestyle of Surrender (with Jeffrey Pelton)

The Sounds of Christmas (with Jeffrey Pelton)

30 DAYS TO BREAKTHROUGH

Becoming Bold and Courageous

30 Days To Breakthrough

Becoming Bold and Courageous

Kathi Pelton
Foreword by Nate Johnston

Becoming Bold and Courageous

© 2019 by Kathi Pelton. All rights reserved.

No part of this publication may be reproduced, stored in a retrieval system, or transmitted in any form or by any means—for example, electronic, photocopy, recording—without the prior written permission of the publisher. The only exception is brief quotations in printed reviews.

Unless otherwise indicated, all Scripture quotations are taken from the Holy Bible, New Living Translation, copyright © 1996, 2004, 2015 by Tyndale House Foundation. Used by permission of Tyndale House Publishers, Inc., Carol Stream, Illinois 60188. All rights reserved.

Scripture quotatations marked (NIV) are taken from the Holy Bible, New International Version®, NIV®. Copyright ©1973, 1978, 1984, 2011 by Biblica, Inc.™ Used by permission of Zondervan.

Scripture quotations marked (AMP) are taken from the Amplified Bible, Copyright © 1954, 1958, 1962, 1964, 1965, 1987 by The Lockman Foundation. Used by permission.

Scripture quotations taken from The Message. Copyright © 1993, 1994, 1995, 1996, 2000, 2001, 2002. Used by permission of NavPress Publishing Group.

Editor and Creative Consultant: Jeffrey Pelton, www.jeffreypelton.com
Cover Design by Pelton Media Group, Portland, OR

First edition
ISBN 978-1-7327707-4-4

Published by Inscribe Press LLC, Tigard, OR

Dedication

This book is dedicated to Keith Green and Daniel Cervi—two men whose boldness to preach the gospel of grace without compromise became the voices that introduced me to the unconditional love of Jesus Christ.

In Keith's short twenty-eight years on this planet he impacted more lives than most people who live to be one hundred. His music and message revealed to me the one who had died to set me free and called me to be His bride.

Daniel dared to take the gospel to my high school campus and then left the ninety-nine to come and find the one—me! I am eternally grateful that he had eyes to see beyond my "lost life" to discover the heart that desperately wanted to be found.

I'm putting Your armor on;
finding myself so suddenly drawn,
like a moth to a flame whenever I hear Your name.
Help me to follow through,
make every day a devotion to You....
(Keith Green, "Dust to Dust")

Contents

Series introduction by Jeffrey Pelton
Foreword by Nate Johnston

1 Removing the Rulership of Fear	1
2 Shake Off Fear	7
3 "Come and do What You Want to Do"	11
4 Still Waters	15
5 A Fresh Start	19
6 You are Not Alone	23
7 The Lord Turns our Darkness into Light	27
8 No Longer Orphans	33
9 You are Always Welcome	37
10 Life is a Gift	41
11 You are Fully Known and Fully Loved	45
12 Learning to Lean on Your Beloved	49
13 Wonderfully Wrecked by His Love	53
14 The Weight of His Glory	57
15 Receiving the Anointing of Purity	61
16 Revived Through Wisdom	65
17 The Voice that Brings Freedom	71
18 God Will Do What You Cannot	77
19 Wrestle Until God Wins	81
20 Boldly Say Yes	85
21 Bold Obedience!	89
22 Going Deeper	95
23 You are an Overcomer	99

24 Your 10:10 Turnaround	105
25 The Path that Overflows	109
26 It's Time for Crazy Courage!	115
27 Great are You Lord	121
28 In My Weakness, You are Strong	125
29 God's Fire on Your Offering	129
30 The Lion of Judah	133
Sources	137

Series Introduction: Thirty Days to What?

This book is part of a series called *30 Days to Breakthrough*. Why thirty days? Is there something special about that length of time? Is there an obscure biblical mandate that we have unearthed in one of the prophetic books of Scripture? Or, is this some sort of spacey, New Age thinking?

The short answer, in acceptable "Christianese," is that God originally spoke to Kathi several years ago about stepping into a new lifestyle of peace by spending thirty days allowing Him to change her thinking, taking her into a new realm of trust in Him.

This is consistent with many psychological studies about human behavior, although there is a great deal of disagreement among experts as to the length of time required to truly change a habit and form a new one. In fact, a lot of recent evidence suggests that it takes a minimum of sixty-six days to truly make a solid difference in a person's life. What everyone can agree on, however, is that changing takes intentionality and effort, and setting aside a specified period for readjustment can be extremely helpful in making the commitment to change. Thirty days may not magically catapult you into a new lifestyle, but it is definitely long enough to get a good jump start.

That is the reason for what you are about to read. This book, *Becoming Bold and Courageous,* is the second book in the series. The more we allow the Holy Spirit to impart His character and fruit in us, the greater our trust in His goodness becomes and we find ourselves responding to Him, rather than reacting to circumstances and trouble around us. The *Thirty*

Days volumes are meant to aid the bride of Christ in her quest to discover and experience more of her beloved Bridegroom and find comfort by trusting more deeply in His care. You can choose to run through the following pages in a session or two, or go through them day-by-day, or dip into some chapter when you feel inspired to read. Any way you approach the material, you will obtain the benefits that come from connecting with another person's journey into the mystery and majesty of walking with our great, eternal Lord. One of the values of Christian teaching and literature is that we are afforded the opportunity to discover how others have walked the roads we all must travel. It is a little like reading someone's diary.

So, enjoy the travelogue. Kathi shares many personal stories and prophetic insights she has gained walking with Jesus. She writes of biblical truths she has learned to "flesh out" in the rough-and-tumble of her daily life on this planet. You will read about failures and triumphs, sorrows and joys, and the richness of life lived as part of the magnificent domain we call the kingdom of God.

~Jeffrey Pelton

Foreword

Six years ago our world went into a spiral without any notice at all.

I received a call at work from Christy, saying she wasn't coping and didn't know what was happening to her. I rushed home in a panic to find her sitting in a daze and the kids crying. What was going on? It felt like a dark cloud had descended on us and I was less than unprepared. That was the first day of a year that felt like we were walking through the valley of the shadow of death, as Christy woke up daily to the formidable onslaught of the enemy against her mind and calling. When we tried to reach out to pastors and leaders, friends—anyone!—we found that none knew how to deal with what we were facing. We were out of our depth and sinking quickly. Now we weren't spiritual novices by any means, but this fight was nothing we had ever faced. After months of doctors' visits not giving any us answers and our lives falling deeper into disarray, we both fell in a heap at the feet of Jesus and finally gave up. "It's about time" the Holy Spirit said back to me.

We decided we weren't going to take this demonic assignment anymore, so we began worshipping every night and speaking and declaring the Word of God together. This would last up to four hours a night at times, contending and warring, declaring and praying, until something would shift and she felt peaceful enough to sleep. Somehow in the middle of it all, God was calling us up to a higher level of authority and teaching us to fight for the territory that lay in front of us.

We were getting somewhere, and we weren't going to give up.

I love the analogy of the chicken and the egg. In order for the chicken to be hatched, it has to apply pressure on the shell from the inside. Many times, we pray for God to burst into our situations and rescue us when He is saying, "You have me inside you; try letting me out."

In that same way, we see now how God wanted Christy and me to begin declaring and speaking to our obstacles. There is something about grabbing the Word of God and speaking out truth that destroys the lies of the enemy. Christy started doing that about six months into her ordeal, and she began to see dramatic results.

One December morning, just over eleven months from when all this began, I was getting ready for work, and our girls were watching a cartoon called *How the Lion Found His Roar*. It got my attention. The story was about the lion who was the king of the jungle but was a pushover because he didn't know how to roar. The animals in the jungle didn't respect him, because he didn't know who he was, and he didn't know how to do what he was born to do. This continued until he found a cave where his forefathers had been and saw drawings there portraying stories of courage and bravery. Suddenly, he discovered who he was and began to roar.

I knew watching this was no coincidence for me. I felt a burst of hope in my spirit and said to myself, *This is the day it ends.*

That night in worship, it felt so hard to press in. Christy was still being mentally tormented and struggling against demonic oppression that plagued her mind. That night, she felt a physical, dark presence surrounding her. After worshipping a long while, we were about to just go to bed when I remembered the cartoon from that morning and the words I had proclaimed: "This is the day it ends." So I told Christy about the lion who had found his roar, and it gave her renewed strength. She grabbed her Bible, as she had done many nights before, clinging to the highlighted Scriptures that become her food each night for almost a year. She began to decree them.

Something happened next that I cannot quite explain. As she was speaking out the Scriptures, it was if they were her own words—she owned them—and then suddenly I watched as she closed her eyes and began prophesying over herself with authority and power; it was like the sound of a loud, deafening roar in the spirit, and we both heard the sound of demons shrieking in terror, as she declared, "For every day you tormented me, Satan, you will pay! You will pay for what you put me through. I am a daughter of the King, and you messed with the wrong person!"

Then complete silence and peace fell on the room. We stared at each other for a few moments in awe, and knew that it had broken. The year-long battle was over, and she was free!

Isaiah 61:1 says,

> *The Spirit of the Lord God is upon me, because the Lord has anointed me to preach good news to the poor; He has sent me to heal the broken-hearted, to proclaim liberty to the captives, and the opening of the prison to those who are bound.*

There is something that happens when you are in a corner. It causes you to either crumble more or to dig deep and tap into your spirit man. When David was in a corner after losing everything at Ziklag, it caused him to run into the presence of God and the rest is history. It's that place of complete dependence and surrender to God that awakens us to the reality of who we really are and what we carry. It's those low places in the battle when all seems lost that we can become acquainted with the Lion of the tribe of Judah that fights for us and THROUGH us. As we see Him fight through us, we find that mighty courage and breakthrough anointing we have always carried!

Being a father and husband, I have had many moments where there is no one around to rescue me in crisis and I've had to look at the giant in front of me and dig deep into my spiritual artillery and pull out a stone to hurl at my enemy. "God has not given me a spirit of fear but power and love and a sound mind!" I have declared this so many times when facing so many doubts and fears warring at my mind. It's those moments that what we have feasted on becomes our defence and our sure victory so we can not only live free, but live as overcomers: undefeatable, strong, mighty, and courageous.

I believe this is such a key topic on the Father's heart for the body of Christ in this season because he doesn't want you and me constantly living underneath our circumstances, laying bloodied and broken in the trenches of a war He has already won. It's time you and I discover who God has called us to be and train daily to live "in Christ in heavenly places."

With that said, I am so excited for you to dive into the pages of this book and feast on its nourishing revelation and drink from its refreshing streams until every fibre of your being is awoken to your full stature in Christ, and hell begins to regret the day it ever messed with you. Kathi has been such a support and friend to us over the years; she is not just a prophet but a true mother to the nations, and as you read this book you will feel nurtured and "hugged" into the deeper places of your destiny. As you walk through the chapters, give yourself space to sit a while and let Kathi's rich "fire-walked" journey lead you into fresh encounters of His love, security, peace, comfort, and pursuing passion.

It's time for you to roar.

~Nate Johnston
Everyday Revivalists
https://nateandchristy.co

Let us therefore come boldly unto the throne of grace, that we may obtain mercy, and find grace to help in time of need.
Hebrews 4:16

BOLDNESS (Parrhesia):

- confidence, fearlessness, freedom of speech
- fearless before danger
- showing or requiring a fearless daring spirit
- willingness to take risks and act innovatively; confidence or courage
- the quality of having a strong, vivid, or clear appearance

1

Removing the Rulership of Fear

At the beginning of this journey to reclaim, rediscover, or newly discover the boldness that is given to all who have put their confidence in Christ, we will first begin to dismantle one of the main oppositions against the believer: fear. It is difficult to live boldly when you are gripped by fear and ruled by a spirit of torment. The answer to living in fear of circumstances is found in the fear of the LORD, which is where we find our hope, our confidence, and His perfect love. From that confident posture we receive boldness to live lives that makes our God known to a lost and fallen world.

Fear can generate terrible chaos in a person's life. It is often the trigger that causes people to make rash decisions, to leave relationships or enter them unwisely, to react in self-protection, to fight or take flight, or to attempt to take control over their environment and circumstances through human reasoning.

Fear is one of satan's favorite weapons against mankind. He eagerly visits individuals and works with countless forms of fear to create triggers—reactions—in "land mines" of poor choices and inflamed emotions existing in the lives of believers and unbelievers alike. The individuals learn, through stepping on these land mines of fear, how to reorder their steps to avoid these explosive traps. Many people literally plan their lives in an attempt to avoid fear, and yet the entire time they are allowing fear to write their narrative and navigate their every step.

Has fear been ruling and dictating your life? Has it replaced the bold and confident steps of those who walk in the fear of the Lord with tiptoeing through your days, in order to keep from awakening the monster called fear that lurks beneath the surface of your soul? If so, take hope, because God is about to remove the ruler called "Fear" from the throne of your life.

It is important to understand that the spirit of fear comes in many different forms that the enemy has custom-designed just for you. The triggers that these fears create become familiar; creating a "cause and effect" that perpetuate ongoing negative cycles in your life. These fears cause reactions that affects decisions, and the direction of your life slowly becomes aligned with demonic agendas that are contrary to God's plans for your life.

ESTABLISHING WHO WILL RULE

Here are some tools that God has given us to enable us to come out from under the rulership of fear:

Ask the Holy Spirit to make you aware of the triggers that cause you to change your steps or actions to accommodate fear. Repent—turn away—from allowing fear to rule over your life and invite the Lord to take His rightful place in those areas that fear has held you captive.

Stop allowing fear to narrate your life. When you feel those familiar fears come knocking at the door of your mind and emotions, immediately stop and renounce partnership and agreement with fear. Then ask the Holy Spirit to replace it with the "fear of the Lord."

Since we have these promises, beloved, let us cleanse ourselves from every defilement of body and spirit, bringing holiness to completion in the fear of God. 2 Corinthians 7:1

The fear of the Lord is a positive, rather than a negative,

fear. Within the life of the one has put their full trust in the Lord there is great freedom and boldness to walk upon the paths that He has prepared for them. Choosing the posture of living in reverence to God, walking in the fear of the Lord and all His ways, allows you to experience the blessings of abundant life.

In the March 1986 issue of Christianity Today, William D. Eisenhower wrote an article titled "Fearing God." He explained how our viewpoints and presuppositions are often completely at odds with the truth revealed to us from Scripture.

> *Unfortunately, many of us presume that the world is the ultimate threat and that God's function is to offset it. How different this is from the biblical position that God is far scarier than the world.... When we assume that the world is the ultimate threat, we give it unwarranted power, for in truth, the world's threats are temporary. When we expect God to balance the stress of the world, we reduce him to the world's equal .... As I walk with the Lord, I discover that God poses an ominous threat to my ego, but not to me. He rescues me from my delusions, so he may reveal the truth that sets me free. He casts me down, only to lift me up again. He sits in judgment of my sin, but forgives me nevertheless. Fear of the Lord is the beginning of wisdom, but love from the Lord is its completion.*

As you choose the fear of the Lord over the rulership by all other fears; you receive freedom from the paths that have led countless others away from true holiness. The holiness of God cleanses His people from the defilement that the fear of man and the fear of any created thing has brought into the lives of many believers. A friend once told me that the Holy Spirit spoke these words to her, *"Any fear but the fear of the Lord is idolatry."*

This is a profound statement of deep truth. Any reaction or emotion that usurps and replaces absolute dependency and trust in Jesus, including fear, becomes idolatry. Jesus alone is your refuge, and within the "shadow of His wing" you can live in boldness and confident assurance. The fear of the Lord is your true protection. It protects you from the sinful nature that once ruled over your life and it protects you from every weapon that the enemy forms against you.

Psalm 91 begins with this confident declaration,

Those who live in the shelter of the Most High will find rest in the shadow of the Almighty. This I declare about the Lord: He alone is my refuge, my place of safety; he is my God, and I trust him.

The deceptions of the enemy are designed to cause you to leave the refuge of trust in God and return to the harsh dictatorship of fears that tempt you away from trust in God alone. This fear will defile you and cause you to become a walking target for the weapons that the enemy has been forming against your life. There is a promise for those who live in the fear of the Lord and place Him alone as their refuge,

If you make the Lord your refuge, if you make the Most High your shelter, no evil will conquer you; no plague will come near your home. For he will order his angels to protect you wherever you go. (Psalms

Today is the day to begin to live in the fear of the Lord. The spirit of fear has been ruling over too many of God's people for far too long. It is time to exchange the fears that have chased us down like hunted deer for the fear of the Lord that provides protection, purity, peace, and holiness. He waits to be invited into the prisons we have been held in by negative fears. He will set us free as we posture our lives in reverence and absolute trust in Him alone.

There is no fear in love. But perfect love casts out fear... (1 John 4:18)

Invite the fear of the Lord and the joy of His perfect love to have full reign in your life today.

Day 1 Declaration

When you lie down, you will not be afraid; when you lie down, your sleep will be sweet. Have no fear of sudden disaster or of the ruin that overtakes the wicked, for the Lord will be at your side and will keep your foot from being snared. (Proverbs 3:24-26)

Today I declare that I put my confidence in the truth that the Lord is always at my side and He is the one who keeps me from disaster. I renounce and repent of the idolatry of fear that has ruled over my soul. I declare that the Lord is now washing me clean from the defilement that has touched me as I have allowed fear to take the place of trust.

I now replace those fears that have driven me from following His voice with the fear of the Lord that protects me and makes me holy. I receive the Lord as my refuge for He is the One my heart fully trusts. I declare that I will now listen to the voice of God rather than the voices that have come to keep my feet from walking upon His chosen paths for my life. Where He leads, I will follow with bold confidence in His unfailing love and goodness.

2

Shake Off Fear

Fear is one of the biggest enemies of mankind; fear drives countless individuals to rely on their own ability to self-protect rather than trust in God. Fear is also one of the best ways to remove boldness and confidence from the life of the believer. If the enemy can terrify you into living according to the fears that plague you rather than in the fear of the Lord, then he has affectively paralyzed you from releasing bold prayers and living in the confident assurance of your faith in Jesus Christ.

Every day affords opportunities that can create moments that induce fear. There are events happening around our world all the time that we have no control over. Yet, the Lord assures us that our eternal hope is unshakable; for no one can separate us from His love or the gift of salvation that He has given to all who have believed. As you learn to live in the grip of your eternal hope and joy, it begins to allow you to shake off all other fears that came to redirect your steps, influence your decisions and narrate your perspective away from God's view. The "things of this world" are shaking around you but you are invited to live as a part of an unshakable kingdom that is eternal. Fear calls out to you from the mouth of the "god of this world," seeking to steal any effectiveness that would be carried out as you live boldly in the fear of the Lord. If you take the hand of fear it becomes the unlocked door for the thief to enter through. The thief that comes with terror to kill, steal and destroy will effectively rob you of the abundant life that is promised to those who walk in the fear of the Lord.

The thief's purpose is to steal and kill and destroy. My purpose is to give them a rich and satisfying life. (John 10:10)

God is inviting you to wake up each new day and form a habit of exchanging the fears that have previously robbed you of joy, peace, and hope for the fear of the Lord that brings you wisdom, refuge, goodness and blessings. The Word of God is filled with the amazing benefits and blessings bestowed upon those who walk in the fear of the Lord. It is time for the Church to evict the thief; closing and locking the door of fear that is allowing the enemy to gain access to their lives. Fear seeks to reorder the steps of the righteous, but for the one who lives in the fear of the Lord, He will order and establish their steps according to His good and perfect plan. The believer following the leading of the Holy Spirit can experience the favor and protection of the Lord even in troubling circumstances.

When the apostle Paul was traveling to Rome under guard, the ship he traveled on was caught in a dreadful storm at sea, and ultimately destroyed on the rocks of the island of Malta. By a miracle of God, everyone aboard was able to reach land safely, and they were aided by the island's inhabitants as they sought to find shelter and dry out before a fire.

Once safely on shore, we found out that the island was called Malta. The islanders showed us unusual kindness. They built a fire and welcomed us all because it was raining and cold. Paul gathered a pile of brushwood and, as he put it on the fire, a viper, driven out by the heat, fastened itself on his hand...But Paul shook the snake off into the fire and suffered no ill effects. (Acts 28:1-3, 5)

Today is a day to shake off the fears that have hindered you and put them under your feet. There is a fear that places your life above every natural fear and enemy; that is the fear of the Lord. From that posture, peace and righteousness will lead you and rule over your life with truth and justice. Shake off that snake called fear and trample it under your feet! Today is your day to boldly and fearlessly take back your joy and trust in Him alone.

Day 2 Declaration

How blessed is everyone who fears the LORD, who walks in His ways. When you shall eat of the fruit of your hands, you will be happy and it will be well with you. Your wife shall be like a fruitful vine within your house, your children like olive plants around your table. Behold, for thus shall the man be blessed who fears the LORD. (Psalm 128:1-4)

But blessed is the one who trusts in the LORD, whose confidence is in him. (Jeremiah 17:17)

Today I declare that the fear of the Lord will be the standard that I live by. I shake off all other fears that have directed my steps away from the path that the Lord has for me to walk upon. I choose this day to walk in His ways and in the confidence given to me by the Holy Spirit. I will walk boldly in the fear of the Lord, knowing that I am a part of an unshakable kingdom that has no end. It is God who directs my steps and keeps my feet from falling.

You, oh God, are the One who makes me fruitful and gives me joy. As I lay down my fears to boldly follow you, I am blessed in all my ways. I put my trust in you and my confidence is in you alone. Take back all that belongs to you and replace the fears that have caused me to have an anxious heart with your perfect love that gives me peace.

3

"Come and Do What You Want to Do!"

So often, in our prayers and in our worship, we submit ourselves and consecrate our lives afresh to the Lord, saying, *"Come and do what you want to do."* But then, when He begins to move us into new realms and unfamiliar experiences, we shrink back in fear. The new and the unfamiliar can reveal where we are still trusting in our own abilities and strengths, rather than relying fully upon His Spirit at work in us.

> *For God has not given us a spirit of fear or timidity, but of power, love and self-discipline (self-control).(2 Timothy 1:7)*

Fear and timidity rob us of the bold confidence we experience when we are fully trusting in the Lord. The Spirit of the Lord lives within us, and the more we yield to Him, the more He is able to do in us those exploits that are beyond our natural ability to accomplish. Because He lives within, greatness resides in us! Doing the things we are easily able to do does not require dependency, but reaching for the great and the impossible requires absolute dependency. It also requires bold confidence; not in ourselves but in Him. We all deal with natural fears, but we must encourage ourselves like Moses did Joshua in Deuteronomy 31,

"Be strong and of good courage, for you must go with this people to the land which the Lord has sworn to their fathers to

give them, and you shall cause them to inherit it. And the Lord, He is the One who goes before you. He will be with you, He will not leave you nor forsake you; do not fear nor be dismayed."

The Lord goes before us; He will be with us and He will never forsake us. We can say with renewed courage, *"Come and do what you want to do in and through my life!"* Greatness rarely comes apart from risk; from moving beyond the comforts of the familiar. We must receive commissioning into the supernatural and impossible realms where we decrease and see His increase. As believers we live in a divine partnership with the God who doesn't need us, but who desires us. He loves to reveal His love, power, and faithfulness through mortal men who have yielded to His Spirit. His greatness is revealed as He is enthroned upon our lives.

When I married my husband, I was so excited because he was comfortable in front of people and didn't mind going on stage to sing and speak. I thought that I would be the supportive wife who sat safely in the crowd. Then, much to my surprise—and distress at the time—God called me to write to public audiences, speak at conferences and gatherings, and prophesy from a stage. I had crippling stage fright, reminding me of my fear of heights. Standing on a stage was like jumping out of a plane, causing me to tremble and experience feelings of dread and terror. But the Lord would say to me, "Be strong and courageous! I am with you and will move through you."

Honestly, it was one of the hardest things I ever faced, but as I trusted in Him, I began to experience the promise of His presence and power amid my fear and weakness. I don't know if it that was the result of any gifting as much as it was about surrendering in obedience to what God called me to do. Remember, He used a donkey to speak to Balaam (Numbers 22:28) and those are animals known for their stubbornness. If He can use a donkey to relay His message, then He surely can use you and me. Sometimes you must stand in the face of your greatest fears to see His greatness revealed.

Day 3 Declaration

*Whenever I am afraid, I will trust in You.
In God (I will praise His word)
In God I have put my trust; I will not fear.
What can flesh do to me? (Psalm 56:3-4)*

I declare this day that when I am afraid, I will put my trust in you! You have called me into your greatness and I say, "Come and do what you want to do, Lord!" You are with me and you will never leave me. When I tremble in my flesh I will go to the unshakable place of surrender. I invite you to display your greatness in and through my life as I put my trust in you.

4

Still Waters

One morning I received a text from a friend that included a lovely photo of the still waters in the harbor that she lives on. She had written, "Be still and know that I am God."

What she did not know was that I had gone uneasily to bed the night before, wrestling in my soul against concerns that were out of my control. Whenever this happens, I am aware that the "stirring of the waters" of my soul is designed to steal my peace, disrupt my stillness (which is the posture of trust, abiding in His faithfulness), and create striving. The enemy comes with whispers of confusion and tumult in order to make waves and block my view of Jesus. When Jesus told Peter to come to Him upon the water, they were on a stormy sea with waves that easily hindered Peter's view of the Lord's outstretched hand. As the waves blocked his view, fear set in and Peter began to sink beneath the raging sea. This is such a clear illustration of what the enemy tries to do with the storms of life and the waves of circumstances.

The one who calms the seas still calls "Come!" to His people. He beckons us to step out of the "boat" of natural understanding into a supernatural walk on the water of faith, but our adversary desires to stir the waters of fear, attempting to block our view of the Lord, so that we will sink under the powerful forces of the natural realm, trading our hope in the unseen for what we see before us, abandoning trust for fear. But God speaks over the storms of life, "Peace be still"; He speaks over your life, "Be still and know that I am God."

Our faith in this truth calms the storms of our souls and takes us into supernatural ability to walk upon water. Faith makes a pathway in which we can walk out to take hold of the outstretched hand of the one who has authority over every natural, created thing.

> *"The LORD is on my side; I will not fear. What can man do to me?" (Psalm 118:6)*

Still waters are a beautiful picture of the peace and mercy the Lord offers us. In the placid quietness, we are refreshed and we are able to refresh our parched souls with the water of His presence. Dwelling beside peaceful waters is a calming and comforting posture.

Do not fear! If God is for us then who can stand against us? Who can stop the Lord Almighty? No one! Speak in faith to your soul, "Be still." Walk out on the water, right in the middle of the natural storm that surrounds you, and trust that you will not sink beneath the waves that rage with fearful intimidations of doom. Take hold of the outstretched hand of Jesus who will lift you above the natural into supernatural stillness, peace, and rest as you walk with Him and abide in the shadow of His wing

> *"He who dwells in the secret place of the Most High Shall abide under the shadow of the Almighty. I will say of the LORD, "He is my refuge and my fortress; My God, in Him I will trust."*

> *He shall cover you with His feathers, And under His wings you shall take refuge; His truth shall be your shield and buckler. You shall not be afraid of the terror by night, Nor of the arrow that flies by day, Nor of the pestilence that walks in*

darkness, Nor of the destruction that lays waste at noonday. A thousand may fall at your side, And ten thousand at your right hand; But it shall not come near you. Only with your eyes shall you look, And see the reward of the wicked.

Because you have made the LORD, who is my refuge, Even the Most High, your dwelling place, No evil shall befall you, Nor shall any plague come near your dwelling; For He shall give His angels charge over you, To keep you in all your ways. In their hands they shall bear you up, Lest you dash your foot against a stone. You shall tread upon the lion and the cobra, The young lion and the serpent you shall trample underfoot.

"Because he has set his love upon Me, therefore I will deliver him; I will set him on high, because he has known My name. He shall call upon Me, and I will answer him; I will be with him in trouble; I will deliver him and honor him. With long life I will satisfy him, And show him My salvation." (Psalms 91:1-2, 4-16)

Day 4 Declaration

Today I declare that the fear of the Lord will be the standard that I live by. I shake off all other fears that have directed my steps away from the path that the Lord has for me to walk upon. I choose this day to walk in His ways and in the confidence given to me by the Holy Spirit. I will walk boldly in the fear of the Lord, knowing that I am a part of an unshakable kingdom that has no end. It is God who directs my steps and keeps my feet from falling.

You, oh God, are the One who makes me fruitful and gives me joy. As I lay down my fears to boldly follow you, I am blessed in all my ways. I put my trust in you and my confidence is in you alone. Take back all that belongs to you and replace the fears that have caused me to have an anxious heart with your perfect love that gives me peace.

5

A Fresh Start

What do you think about when you wake up and begin each day? Are you encouraged by the presence of God who loves you, or do you feel a mild oppression and a sense of unease?

One day I was taken into a vision where the Lord showed me a large whiteboard filled with words:

words of accusation (some true and some false)
words that recounted past failures and shortcomings
words that spoke wrong identity
words that brought captivity
words that declared condemnation

As I stood reading, Jesus came and washed the whiteboard clean until it was pure and white once again. His mercy and truth swept away the words of accusation and defilement (Romans 8:1; Colossians 2:13-14). If you have faced this "whiteboard" in your life, what awaits you today is a fresh start.

The enemy mocks God's people with relentless accusations and condemnation, but Jesus comes and erases every word that has become a weapon formed against you. These weapons are designed to steal your peace, your joy, your identity in Christ—and most of all, the intimacy with Him that transforms you. When these things are stolen the believer loses his or her confidence and will cease approaching the Lord with boldness. But God, in His relentless love, removes every stain and pursues you with a constant longing to be one with you and to wash away every guilty stain.

I have discovered that every word that comes from my precious Jesus draws me close to Him—even the words of correction that lead me to repentance—for they usher me into new freedoms. His words always break down my walls of shame, revealing His love and true nature. His words wash me and wash over me like ocean waves upon a beach, that time and time again remove the day's debris. His words awaken me to new life and new depths of His love, as they draw me into that sacred place where deep calls unto deep (Psalm 42:7). His words give me a fresh start morning by morning.

If your mind is cluttered with accusations or reminders of past failures that weigh you down with guilt and condemnation, then invite Jesus to wash it all away. You can boldly approach Him with all the words that have sought to separate you and experience Him covering you with His robes of righteousness. He is your fresh start and His words will set you free to truly live again. He will write His truths upon the canvas of your life and reveal the story that He carefully planned for you before the world began.

Today is your fresh start; today is your new beginning. The waves of His love are washing all the debris away and you can now be overcome by His beauty and His glory and go deeper into the intimacy that comes when all the clutter is removed.

Day 5 Declaration

The faithful love of the Lord never ends! His mercies never cease. Great is his faithfulness; his mercies begin afresh each morning. (Lamentations 3:22-23)

I declare that today is a fresh start and new beginning. All memories of shame and reminders of failures have been washed away in the mercy of God. I am clean, I am clothed in the righteousness of Jesus, and I am stepping out of the captivity of the words that have held me back from approaching Him with bold confidence. I declare that His faithful love never ends and is never lacking.

Nothing that I have done can separate me from the love of Jesus and nothing I do can earn His love. Great is His faithfulness in my life and He is greatly to be praised. I have been washed and given a new, fresh start. My fresh start is separated from fear, condemnation, guilt, and accusation. I am loved and received just as I am.

6

You Are Not Alone

We are all aware there is strength in numbers. We find strength in teams, strength in family, and strength in covenant relationships. Why is this such a universal truth? Because we were not created to be alone but were created for relationships and to belong in family. Even Adam, who lived in a perfect place and in perfect health with his perfect Creator, needed a "helper" (helpmate).

> *"The LORD God said, 'It is not good for the man to be alone' "*
> *Genesis 2:18*

I grew up in a broken family and as a child I envied the strength and confidence carried by my friends who were a part of strong families. It was as though what they received within the bond and unity of family traveled with them into all that they did. They carried themselves better and they achieved more than those of my friends who, like me, were from dysfunctional and broken homes. I longed to experience what they had.

When I met and married my husband, I remember feeling, for the first time, a rest and a confidence that I had never known before. In joining with him, I found the safe place of belonging; it was warmth that I had never known but had always desired. Even when we were apart, I knew that I was not alone because distance could not separate me from his love. It became a beautiful picture of what God desired my relationship with Him to look like.

Whether you are married or not, or have a good family or not, you were not created to be alone. God loves family and His family is meant to provide strength, confidence, warmth, and boldness to every member. The perfect bond of unity within the Godhead gives us all a foundation that cannot be shaken, that holds us together as we walk in the unity we are invited into. Jesus prayed for this in John 17:20-23,

> *"My prayer is not for them alone. I pray also for those who will believe in me through their message, that all of them may be one, Father, just as you are in me and I am in you. May they also be in us so that the world may believe that you have sent me. I have given them the glory that you gave me, that they may be one as we are one— I in them and you in me—so that they may be brought to complete unity. Then the world will know that you sent me and have loved them even as you have loved me..."*

Marriage and family are an earthly representation of a heavenly design. When we come into Christ, we are invited into "oneness with Christ" that removes the loneliness and the waywardness that we experienced before knowing Him. Through God we are given a way to experience this unity with His people as the family that carries His heart and His likeness. His glory makes us one as we allow it to permeate our lives.

But what is the glory of God that makes us one? I love John Piper's definition of God's glory:

> *"...the glory of God is the manifest beauty of his holiness."*

His glory draws us into oneness with Christ, into unity with the Godhead, and into a unified family together with every member of His body. His glory is our only hope for unity, because it takes us from the coldness of being alone into the warmth of being joined together by the manifest beauty of His holiness. There is no loneliness within the Godhead, and we are invited into this beautiful and glorious union. This gives us hope and courage as we move through our lives and face the challenges each day brings.

Day 6 Declaration

Two are better than one, because they have a good return for their labor: If either of them falls down, one can help the other up. But pity anyone who falls and has no one to help them up. Also, if two lie down together, they will keep warm. But how can one keep warm alone? Though one may be overpowered, two can defend themselves. A cord of three strands is not quickly broken. (Ecclesiastes 4:9-12)

Today I declare and receive the glory of God upon my life. I was not created to be separated or divided from oneness with God or with His people. Lord, I invite the "manifest beauty of your holiness" to come upon me now. I intercede and declare the glory of God upon your body so that we will be one as you are one. I am not alone because I was born by the Spirit into a family, and you are a God who puts the lonely in families (Psalm 68:6). I receive the gift of family, the gift of strength that comes from family, the gift of warmth that comes through intimacy, and the unity that your glory brings.

I invite your glory to come upon my family so that we will walk in unity, a unity that makes us bold and causes the world to see you. I will love boldly and live confidently within the beauty of your holiness.

7

The Lord Turns Our Darkness into Light

Our first parents sinned. From the time Adam and Eve disobeyed in the garden of Eden, human beings have always experienced trouble in this world. If you pay attention to news reports from our non-stop, never-at-rest media culture, you will imagine that there just isn't any such thing as good news. These days, it seems as though the stories of natural disasters, horrific crimes, and declining morality are at an all-time high. What is the church to do? Who is ruling the nations?

Do not be discouraged! God is on His throne and His government is the government that is sure and final. We are the people who are governed by His righteous courts and we have the favor of His Kingdom upon us. There will always be trouble and unrest in this world, but we must do as Psalm 95 instructs:

Come, let us bow down in worship, let us kneel before the Lord our Maker."

This is where we find rest, peace, and assurance. This is where we come into agreement with our Creator's governmental rule and reign. This is where we establish His throne on Earth as it is in heaven.

Psalm 95 goes on to warn us not to be like those in past generations who hardened their hearts. We do not want to be a generation of people whose hearts wander astray, but instead be a generation that walks in the light through the midst of great darkness, and worships our faithful King.

Light always dispels darkness and we are portals that allow light to shine into dark places. As we bow down in worship and submit to Jesus as King, we allow His light to be manifest into darkness and into situations that need breakthrough.

> *You, LORD, are my lamp; the LORD turns my darkness into light. With Your help I can advance against a troop; with my God I can scale a wall. (2 Samuel 22:29-30)*

If you have ever worked on any sort of machine with small parts, then you know you need bright light to see what the problem is or to change a part. The same is true in so many of life's situations. It is hard to discern a problem or gain understanding when all you can see is darkness. Light allows you to see problems and how they can be made right again.

I have often found myself called into situations with a team to discern a problem or seek the Lord for direction. I have found that the best way for us to discern is to place ourselves in a posture of worship and submission to Jesus. We begin by praying in the Spirit, worshiping, and declaring Jesus as Lord. We bow before Him and listen for His wisdom.

This posture is like taking out a spotlight and shining it onto a problem. We allow His light and wisdom to lead us in the right direction, with understanding as to what to do. We must be people of the light. We must be people who walk in the light or we will not know what to do or where to go.

In every situation that we need wisdom or direction, the Lord becomes the lamp that turns our darkness into light and allows us to once again advance and overcome every obstacle that stands before us.

Several years ago our son-in-law was in a motorcycle accident that left him needing surgery. The hospitals, labs, ambulance service, and pharmacies did not delay in sending our kids thousands of dollars' worth of bills. They were overwhelmed – both by the loss of work and the medical expenses because of his injuries.

I began to worship, praying for them and listening for the Lord's wisdom and direction. Soon I knew that His light was coming into the situation. By the next morning we were contacted by some of our son-in-law's co-workers who had decided to set up an online fund in his name to help cover the medical expenses. I knew that these people, though not believers, had received divine inspiration from the Lord. We can bring light and direction into situations through our prayers and worship, even where people who are not walking with Him are involved. Within a short time, they had raised all the money that was needed, and more.

To walk with God is to have an Advocate, Counselor, Judge (who always rules in your favor), Financial Advisor, Physician, Friend, and Father with you twenty-four hours a day. He understands that we are merely mortal and are in great need of wisdom and help. He loves to be invited into our lives and circumstances so that we can experience the display of His love on a daily basis

> *I will lead the blind by ways they have not known, along unfamiliar paths I will guide them; I will turn the darkness into light before them and make the rough places smooth. These are the things I will do; I will not forsake them. (Isaiah 42:16)*

I have always been horrible with maps and directions. When technology came out with GPS systems and smart phones with GPS capability, it was a happy day for me, and others like me. Prayer and worship are like turning on our spiritual navigation system day-by-day. By humbling ourselves and honoring Him and reading His Word, we are given directions and wisdom for our journey. Bowing before Him can be a physical action, but it is also a posture of our hearts. This frees the Holy Spirit to always be able to quickly tell us which way to go or how to handle a situation. Sometimes it takes me a while to align my actions with His whispers but once I do, I begin seeing light come in almost instantly.

One night I was driving through Oakland, California on a very confusing part of the freeway with many interchanges and merging highways. It was late and I was tired. I ended up in the wrong lane and had to take an exit which led me onto the Bay Bridge heading straight into San Francisco. I was instantly in a panic because I had missed the proper exit and was now stuck traveling in a direction that was going to take me through the city, which would be long and frustrating. But my GPS quickly recalculated my route, and I drove through the confusing areas of San Francisco more easily than I expected, ending up merging onto an even more familiar route than I had been going before!

Know that if you end up going the wrong direction or making the wrong decision, God can recalculate your route. It may take you a bit longer or cause you a few extra stops or turns, but He is able to make your rough roads smooth and lead you through unfamiliar paths. And who knows, maybe God was keeping me from dangers on the other route!

If you need light in darkness, direction on an unfamiliar path, wisdom, or discernment; now is the time to bow down and worship!

Day 7 Declaration

Come, let us bow down in worship, let us kneel before the LORD our Maker; for He is our God and we are the people of His pasture, the flock under His care.(Psalm 95:6-7)

I declare that you, Jesus, are my light and my salvation! There is no one like you! I bow down to worship you for I am yours. You are my answer to every question, my provision in every need, my healer in every sickness, my compass on life's paths, and my companion when I feel alone. In darkness you are my light and I will not fear. I will worship, pray, and put my trust in you. I am under your care!

8

No Longer Orphans

A life of poverty is a crushing and debilitating condition; a cruel taskmaster, responsible for untold misery and evil. When we consider people in poverty, we usually think of those who lack basic needs and who live in less than desirable conditions. Yet, a spirit of poverty spirit can exist in a person who lives in a mansion, drives a fancy car, and takes extravagant vacations. Underneath the success and glamor, many people suffer and struggle with a feeling of emptiness—of being orphaned and adrift in a cold world—and they are driven to gain security in every way possible. This motivation will often mask itself in greed, which is an intense and selfish desire for something; especially wealth, power, or food.

Greed is addictive and often insatiable. It always needs more and feels a lack even in abundance. Why is this? It is because often greed is just the pain of the emptiness of orphan and poverty mentalities. It may start with a true need but if not dealt with it can quickly become a black hole that can never be filled or satisfied.

Psalm 23 says, "The Lord is my Shepherd, I shall not want…"

There is a filling up and overflow of every good and perfect thing when we become part of our Good Shepherd's flock.

"So don't be afraid, little flock. For it gives your Father great happiness to give you the Kingdom." Luke 12:32

When we come to know Christ as our Savior we become sons and daughters of God. As we fully leave the "orphan spirit"—which walks hand in hand with a spirit of poverty—in order to receive the spirit of sonship, we become aware that we not only are a part of a family but are also joint heirs with the Kingdom of God; a kingdom that has no lack. His Kingdom is filled with abundance, beauty, fruit, resources, relationships, love, and every good and perfect gift.

In the place of sonship our lives go from having our roots planted in a dry and desert land, where there is always lack and thirst, to being planted by streams of refreshing waters and fruitful orchards where we thrive in every season.

Greed often begins in need! The deep need for a father, a family, a place to call home is inherent in every person because that is how God made us. When that need is not met, we take on an orphan spirit that believes that there is no one to watch over them, therefore the person becomes their own self-protector and "self" becomes the focus for the sake of survival. Eventually this "self" focus will take root and give place to greed.

In the Book of Luke, chapter 12:13-21 we read about the parable of the rich fool who stored up his treasures on earth but did not have relationship with God. He stored up an abundance and then decided to live to satisfy the desires of his flesh. That night he died leaving his earthly storehouse behind yet having no heavenly treasure stored up.

"Then he said, "Beware! Guard against every kind of greed. Life is not measured by how much you own."" (Luke 12:15)

The end of this parable says,

"Yes, a person is a fool to store up earthly wealth but not have a rich relationship with God." (Luke 12:21)

Need that is filled outside of a rich relationship with God merely becomes greed that will make you a fool. The person who invests in a rich relationship with God will be a person who gives generously and yet lacks no good thing. That person will be rich in life and when death comes he will have eternal treasures stored up that will have no end.

God desires to give you the gift of sonship which will satisfy you and make you generous in every way. A greedy person becomes an idolater, worshipping the things of this world (Ephesians 5:5), and never being satisfied. As sons and daughters, we have been given the Kingdom of God which lacks nothing. We can give to others in need without fear of being left in want. We can love others more than ourselves without fear of not having our needs met. We can become selfless and still know that we have a Father that watches over every detail of our lives.

Part of the amazing gift that God is giving His people in these days is the gift of freedom that has kept His people from the fullness of sonship. We were not created to live in the grip of "want" that leads to the captivity of greed. If you sense a root of greed that stems from a poverty or orphan spirit then God is reaching out to you to set you free. He will exchange the orphan identity for the identity of a son or daughter. He will exchange the deep fears of poverty and lack for the assurance of His Kingdom that has peace and plenty. He will exchange the greed that never satisfies with the riches of relationship with Him that make you generous. Lastly, He will set you free from being self-focused to being Christ-focused, which will make you a light to the world.

It is His great love that offers you this supernatural exchange!

> *Blessed be the God and Father of our Lord Jesus Chyrist, who has blessed us with every spiritual blessing in the heavenly places in Christ. (Ephesians 1:3)*

Day 8 Declaration

...he predestined us for adoption to sonship through Jesus Christ, in accordance with his pleasure and will— to the praise of his glorious grace, which he has freely given us in the One he loves. (Ephesians 1:5-6)

I declare over my life that I was created for, and predestined to live in, sonship through Jesus. It brings Him pleasure to freely give me all that I was created to inherit. I will no longer identify as those who are "lonely" or "needy" for I have been adopted into His family. Lack is not my inheritance but rather abundance is my portion! Abandonment is not my fate but rather I claim the promise that I am never alone or forsaken! Greed is not part of my condition but instead, generosity and desires fulfilled.

9

You Are Always Welcome

My husband and I have been blessed with three young grandsons (so far). When those boys arrive at Grandpa and Grandma's house, they always know that they will find our arms wide open to embrace them, they know our love will surround them, and they are completely confident that they have entered a safe haven that enfolds them into loving care. Our grandsons never hesitate to boldly rush through the door of our home and into our arms because they have only known love and acceptance in this place where they are welcome.

When I was a child, going to my grandparent's house was a very different experience. My dad would begin by calling his parents in hopes to arrange a visit, only to listen to the sound of their phone ringing over and over with no answer, even though he knew they were home. If by chance they answered they would tell him not to come because my grandmother didn't feel well. Often, my dad would decide to go anyway, without invitation, so he and my mom would pack all three of us kids in the car and we would make the drive in silent anxiety, knowing that when we arrived we would not be welcome. We would pull up in front of the house, my dad would step out of the car, and have us wait while he tried to get his dad to answer the door. He would ring the doorbell, knock loudly on the door, knock on windows, and shout their names. This would go on for what seemed to be hours (although in reality it was probably no more than fifteen minutes). Finally my grandfather would answer the door, scowling with frustration and disapproval as he grudgingly allowed us in, and we would visit with them, knowing all-the-while that we were not welcome.

YOU ARE WELCOME!

These two scenarios create two different types of children; one creates children who are bold and full of joy and the other creates children who are timid and afraid. Satan surely takes pleasure in trying to misrepresent God as someone who will not "take your calls" or open His door to you. He would like you to believe that God only opens the door to you when you relentlessly bother Him enough to get a response. The enemy will even twist Jesus' parables about persistence in prayer to make us think that God doesn't really want to be bothered by us. Yet, the truth is that God is always excited to receive you, His arms and His heart are always open to you, and you are enfolded into the safety of His care day and night. This truth should make you bold and confident to rush to Him whenever you desire. He is never too busy and He never tires of spending time with you. Just as I love to welcome my grandsons and do special things for them, so your heavenly Father is the same toward you.

> *If you then, evil as you are, know how to give good and advantageous gifts to your children, how much more will your Father Who is in heaven [perfect as He is] give good and advantageous things to those who keep on asking Him! (Matthew 7:11)*

Have you believed the wrong narrative regarding how God perceives and receives you? Have you believed that He withholds good things from you and takes pleasure in watching you beg? If so, you have been deceived. God is not a man that

He should tell a lie; therefore, when His Word tells us that He will exceed even the good gifts human parents love to bestow, then you should believe it. Lies and fear about God's heart make many believers timid in approaching Him but He is calling you to come boldly before Him, knowing confidently that you will be received, and trusting that He has "good and advantageous" things to give to you when you ask.

> *God is not a man, that He should tell or act a lie, neither the son of man, that He should feel repentance or compunction [for what He has promised]. Has He said and shall He not do it? Or has He spoken and shall He not make it good? (Numbers 23:19)*

Day 9 Declaration

So let us come boldly to the throne of our gracious God. There we will receive his mercy, and we will find grace to help us when we need it most. (Hebrews 4:16, NLT)

Today, I declare to my soul the truth that I am always welcome in my Father's house and in His arms. I reject every narrative that has come to misrepresent Him as a Father that is aloof, distant, cold, and withholding. Holy Spirit, I ask you to remove the lie that has brought timidity and insecurities into my relationship with you. I receive the spirit of truth that makes me confident in your love toward me, and bold in my approach toward you, because of your great love for me.

I declare that you are not a man that you should lie or withhold that which you have promised. You delight in me and it brings you pleasure to give good and advantageous things to me. All that you have spoken you will make good concerning me. I am always welcome and always wanted by you. Thank you for being such a good, good Father.

10

Life is a Gift

Your life is an astonishing gift, a miracle wrought in the secret place of the protection and covering of your mother's womb. And just like that miracle that brought you to this earth, so were you birthed anew in the womb of God's presence the day you received Christ as your Savior. Our lives here on earth are a time of growing in the understanding and experience of His character, His ways, His truths, and His love. As we grow, we remain in the constant womb of His presence. We are never separated from His love or His protective covering.

> *Whoever dwells in the shelter of the Most High*
> *will rest in the shadow of the Almighty.*
> *I will say of the Lord, "He is my refuge and my fortress,*
>   *my God, in whom I trust." (Psalm 91:1-2)*

As he or she is being marvelously formed, a baby knows no fear or want. The little one's existence and nourishment is fully provided for within the incubator of its mother's womb. It is no different for those who have been conceived into the family of God. Everything that you need is provided for: nourishment, warmth, protection, resource, and love. If a baby in its mother's womb feels no fear, then how much more should we venture into each new day free from fear; bold and courageous within the protection of His presence.

> *Even if my father and mother abandon me, the LORD will hold me close. (Psalme 27:10)*

He gives His angels charge concerning you and every aspect of your life. His Spirit takes up residence within you, fully equipping you with the power that raised Jesus from the dead; and nothing can separate you from His perfect love. It is a love that casts out all fear. A child walking down the street with a loving father holding onto one hand, a nurturing mother holding the other hand, with a full police escort surrounding them, would still not be as safe as you are within the grip of God's love and care.

Yet, so often we let our natural eyes dictate our reality rather than the truth of the Bible. If the Bible is true, and we know it is, then why are we still afraid so often? Shouldn't we be the bravest people on the face of the earth? Shouldn't we have joy and peace in every circumstance? What if we allowed the agape love of God to permeate the conditional love that we've experienced within the constraints of human love? What if we became more aware of the womb of His presence that we live in than the natural world around us? What if we became more acquainted with the angels that surround us than the enemy that accuses us? If we died, surely then we would become bold and courageous, because we would see Him in fullness, and would become unstoppable, fearless, brave, and obedient to everything that He asked of us.

Today we can ask our amazing God to shift how we see and perceive, how we live, how we breathe, and how we believe.

> *'For in Him we live and move and have our being. As some of your own poets have said, 'We are His offspring.' (Acts 17:28)*

You are not an "at risk child" but rather a child of God. Everything you need is found in everything He is! He is in you, beside you, around you, over you, behind you, and before you.

> *Christ be with me, Christ within me,*
> *Christ behind me, Christ before me,*
> *Christ beside me, Christ to win me,*
> *Christ to comfort and restore me.*
> *Christ beneath me, Christ above me,*
> *Christ in quiet, Christ in danger....*
> *(from "St. Patrick's Breastplate")*

Your confidence is in who He is and where He is. He is your good Father; He is your Lord and Savior; He is your ever-present Comforter and He is always with you.

Day 10 Declaration

If you make the Most High your dwelling-- even the LORD, who is my refuge-- then no harm will befall you, no disaster will come near your tent. For he will command his angels concerning you to guard you in all your ways; they will lift you up in their hands, so that you will not strike your foot against a stone. You will tread upon the lion and the cobra; you will trample the great lion and the serpent. "Because he loves me," says the LORD, "I will rescue him; I will protect him, for he acknowledges my name. He will call upon me, and I will answer him; I will be with him in trouble, I will deliver him and honor him. With long life will I satisfy him and show him my salvation." (Psalm 91:9-16)

Today I declare that I will no longer view my life according to the way my natural eyes see but according to the truth revealed in the Word of God. The Lord is my refuge! I am living in the dwelling place of the Most High God where I am kept from harm and disaster. I am guarded by angels in ALL my ways so that I do not stumble. I can face life-threatening moments and because I love Him, He will rescue me, answer me, deliver me, and honor me. This is my reality and how I will view my life and my existence.

11

You Are Fully Known and Fully Loved

As I awoke this morning, I began hearing over and over in my mind and my spirit, "You are fully known and fully loved."

There is nothing hidden from our God and yet as we stand before Him, we need not feel shame, because we know that we are fully and completely loved. In our nakedness, we stand before our Father clothed in the righteousness of His Son. As we become aware of the depths of our weakness we are then empowered by His strength. And as we admit our ignorance of knowing what to do or how to proceed, we are given supernatural wisdom and understanding that makes us look brilliant. For it is in the posture of humble surrender that He exalts us.

We live in an upside-down world that is in direct contrast to the Kingdom of God. In this world you are quickly judged based on physical appearance, worldly wisdom, possessions, talents, power, and influence. Yet even inside people who possess these amazing traits is one core and vital need: to be known and to be loved.

God looks upon what He has made in you and declares, "It is good." He knows whose image you bear and the beauty that has been placed within you. When God asks you to let Him search your heart it is because you are known loved. Because God honors you, He is always searching out what might keep you from the fullness of His plans for you and His love for you. He is a Father who desires the best for you, not a detective seeking to expose you.

I love the fact that I am fully known by Him. I love that there is nothing hidden and nothing too hard for Him. I love that every challenging place for me is an opportunity for His power to move within me. I love that every weak place within me has become the very place that I will see His power manifest. And I love that as I depend on Him, He gives me wisdom that makes me look brilliant. Most of all, I love that I am fully loved by Him.

We are rich because we are fully known and fully loved. No earthly treasure can compare to this; it is the one thing that cannot be stolen. Some may be deceived into believing that if they are known by God that they will not be loved by Him, but it doesn't change that truth that says, "Nothing can separate us from the love of God." Not even being fully known!

As I rest in this truth it stirs within me a deep hunger to know Him more completely. The revelation of who He is and the mysteries of His ways, the glories of His true nature and the wonders of His Kingdom will always be daily gifts offered to us to unwrap. The more I know Him the more I know how greatly I am loved and how thoroughly I am known; and I am unashamed.

He is my goal and my prize. He is my true north and my first love. To know Him more each day is to love Him more every day. The more that I embrace that I am fully known and still fully loved, the more I am restored to His original intent for my life. This understanding takes me back to the garden where, like Adam and Eve, I can stand naked and yet feel no shame.

When I was a child, I used to hide behind a locked bathroom door to escape my father's anger and the chaotic atmosphere that existed in our home. I would go into the bathroom and close the door to hide from life, from people, and from God. I always felt that in that place I was safe from everyone; even

God. Many years later, on a certain day, the Lord asked me to leave the door open and let Him come in. An absolute miracle happened that day; I became aware that I was fully known and still fully loved and as I allowed myself to be known, even in my utter weakness, it created an environment that allowed me to experience His love.

Today our beautiful Father wants you to know that you are fully known and fully loved by Him. He is inviting you into knowing Him more fully. As you accept His invitation you will fall even more in love with Him, and will find yourself bolder than you ever imagined.

Oh what a Savior, oh what a friend. Isn't He wonderful!

Day 11 Declaration

Then God said, "Let Us make man in Our image, according to Our likeness…" So God created human being in his own image. In the image of God he created them; male and female he created them. (Genesis 1:26, 27)

Today I come into the awareness that when I am seen by God, I do not have to be ashamed or try to cover my nakedness. I am created in His image, "according to His likeness"; therefore I am all-together lovely. I declare over my life, "I am fully known and fully loved." I do not have to hide anything from Him or live behind walls of shame because the Lord takes great pleasure in drawing me into His original intent for my life; to display His image.

I choose right now to take off any masks and come out from behind any walls, and I move into the light of His perfect love where I am transformed by His glory. I rejoice that I do not have to hide any part of me from Him and I know that even in my weaknesses, my shortcomings, and my insecurities, I am fully accepted and fully loved.

12

Learning to Lean Upon Your Beloved

Wilderness times are hard, and they are unavoidable in the Christian life. Jesus Himself was led by the Spirit into the wilderness, where He was tested and where He prepared Himself for the great work ahead of Him. In the wilderness, He did not rely on His own strength, but submitted Himself fully to His Father and the Holy Spirit; a posture He maintained continually. Scripture tells us He was weakened and hungry when the devil came to tempt and test Him, but Jesus overcame through His utter dependence on the power of God.

I awoke this morning hearing the verse from Song of Songs,

"Who is this coming up from the wilderness leaning on her beloved?" (Song of Songs 8:5a)

Have you ever been through a long wilderness season? I went through a three-year wilderness time in the late 1990s. It was the hardest time of my life as I navigated my way through what I would call my "dark night of the soul." The amazing thing is that in the most painful and dark time in my journey with Christ I was given the strength to wrestle down the despair that sought to take my life, in order to find the place of "leaning upon my Beloved." Then He carried me out of the wilderness into a vast and open place.

Although God is not the author of despair, it is not foreign to even the most spiritual of men and women. Yet, during wilderness times or dark nights of the soul, there is great hope to be found in dependency and intimacy with our beloved Savior. He does not abandon us in the wilderness but rather He is ever-present to calm our fears, comfort our pain, and invite us into His arms of love.

Though I'd never wish my dark night upon anyone, I am so grateful that God allowed me to go through the wilderness because it was during that time that I was set free from many strongholds and healed of deep wounds from my childhood, and I discovered true intimacy for the first time. It did not come cheaply or easily or without many moments of stumbling over the chains that bound me, but in the end, I found boldness to arise and live an abundant life as I learned to lean upon my Beloved. (You will read more about this time in day twenty-three.)

During the last months of my wilderness time I would hear the words from Songs of Songs flowing through my spirit like a declaration of joy from the throne of God. It was like an announcement of freedom and a completed work in my life. As I came out of the wilderness, leaning with absolute love and dependency upon Jesus, I was greeted with such a heavenly celebration! The next three years became a manifestation of unexpected and undeserved blessings. I had encounters with God that I didn't even know were possible and I walked in a favor that was unexplainable

Let the sweet words from Song of Songs 8:5 wash over you. These words are for everyone who has been through a long wilderness time, because He is drawing you into the beauty of dependency and intimacy. You must enter bold trust and let all self-sufficiency fall away in the midst of the darkness and pain. It is there that you learn to lean upon your Beloved.

You too have a celebration of heavenly encounters awaiting you. An open land awaits you that is filled with favor, desires fulfilled, and great restoration. As you reject the fate that the enemy has sought to put upon you through this difficult time and you have held onto the promises of your inheritance in Christ Jesus, you will be strengthened and prepared to remain pure in the abundant blessings He has in store for you.

I encourage you to "choose life." This was a key element for my freedom. I had to reject death and destruction and choose life during a time that I just wanted the pain to end.

Whatever the wilderness, wherever the wilderness, it is in that wilderness where we learn that we do not live by bread alone but by every word that proceeds from the mouth of God, that His word is not only most natural food for our soul but the most necessary. (Ken Gire, Windows of the Soul)

In the wilderness I found that the Lord was my life and every other thing fell away. Nothing saved me but Him. As I chose life, I chose Christ! Prior to the wilderness I had many things that I chose to comfort me, to fill the empty places instead of Christ alone. As they fell away during my three years in the wilderness, I found Him to be my all-sufficiency. I learned to lean upon my Beloved and desire Him alone. After that, other blessings were added but they did not take His place.

I finish with this as a prayer for you:

"Place me like a seal over your heart, like a seal on your arm; for love is as strong as death, its jealousy unyielding as the grave. It burns like blazing fire, like a mighty flame. Many waters cannot quench love; rivers cannot sweep it away. If one were to give all the wealth of one's house for love, it would be utterly scorned." (Song of Songs 8:6-7)

Day 12 Declaration

Deuteronomy 30:19-20 "This day I call the heavens and the earth as witnesses against you that I have set before you life and death, blessings and curses. Now choose life, so that you and your children may live and that you may love the Lord your God, listen to his voice, and hold fast to him. For the Lord is your life, and he will give you many years in the land he swore to give to your fathers, Abraham, Isaac and Jacob."

Today I boldly choose life! I choose blessings and I reject death and curses. Though I have faced seasons that have been dark and painful, I choose to yield into the posture of leaning upon my Beloved in the wilderness times. I reject leaning upon my understanding, or upon any comfort but the comfort that comes from absolute trust in my Beloved. I ask now for that seal to be put upon my heart; the seal of your love and the fierce jealousy you feel over having all of me. I lean upon you now, Jesus. You are faithful and will uphold me!

13

Wonderfully Wrecked by His Love

Do you know how very much your heavenly Father loves you? It would wonderfully wreck you if you understood this boundless and intense passion. I pray for you to be wrecked in the most wonderful and glorious way today; wrecked by the revelation and experience of His love for you.

Recently, I sat alone with the Lord and just let His love hold me and wash over me, overwhelming me in the most wonderful way. His love toward me exceeded my love for my own children (which seem immeasurable) and at the same time fully encompasses my love for them. There was no separation; His love permeated all that I love. I didn't have to do anything or say anything. I merely had to stop long enough to let Him be my "Daddy."

During this time, I became acutely aware that He did not care about my flaws or my imperfections; He just adored me for who I was. He wanted me to know how much He loved me and how safe it is to be vulnerable with Him. His love for me covered everything and everyone that I love with a greater love than I can give.

And that is how He feels about you. He adores you! He desires to draw you into the safety of His care, the bounty of His provisions, and the beauty of the garden of His never-failing love. There are moments where God merely wants you to bask in His delight for you. He does not want you to do anything except be still and allow Him to be your Father. He wants to relieve you from the weights that you've been carrying that can drive you to try to earn His favor through works and performance, placing heavy burdens on you. His grace and love will draw you back into the security of a son or daughter; relieving you from the old and all-too-familiar places where orphans fend for themselves and work for acceptance.

We were created for dependency upon someone bigger and stronger than we are. We are sons and daughters; no longer orphans or those who have been forsaken.

You will never be more loved than you are at this very moment. No works, no righteous deeds, no successes will cause Him to love you more. You can stand before Him with all your strengths and weaknesses, your gifts and your inabilities, your beauty and your depravity, and none of that will add to or subtract from His unfathomable and never-changing love for you. You can boldly stand naked and unashamed; knowing that you stand in robes of righteousness through the grace of Jesus Christ.

You are loved beyond measure and cherished beyond imagination. It is within the realms and reality of His love that we become renewed with boldness. Well-loved children run boldly into the arms of their father and they go out into the world with the confidence that being loved provides. It is time for you to be wonderfully wrecked by His love. May your offering today be to offer you: let Him love you, let Him wreck you, and let Him adore you in the way that He longs to. Will you offer Him your surrender? Will you offer Him your dependency? Will you offer Him "you"—just as you are?

Day 13 Declaration

"How great is the love the Father has lavished on us that we should be called children of God!" (1 John 3:1)

I declare that my life is fully yielded to you today, Jesus. Every part of me needs your love to permeate it. I come to you boldly with all my strengths and weaknesses, knowing that I am fully loved and fully received because of the greatness of your love and the price that Jesus paid to reconcile me to you. I offer myself to you and know that I am your child who is greatly loved. Wreck me with your wondrous love and let me desire nothing more than to belong to you. I receive the adoration that you want to lavish me with. I declare that I am your daughter or son and I receive the full benefit of having you as my Father.

14

The Weight of His Glory

When God speaks, bad reports become praise reports. When God moves, dark waves become still waters. When God blesses, small offerings are multiplied into abundant supply. When God touches, the blind see and the lame dance. When God commands, mountains move and a pathway is created. When God delivers, demons flee and men are restored.

When God loves, broken lives are forever changed!

Every day with God is a day of miracles. Whatever your need is today, there is abundant provision and wisdom available in Him. No matter how big or how small, how crucial or how trivial your situation may be; He loves to speak, move, bless, deliver, and love you. As we have been discussing in this book, it is vital that we understand His power to deliver us and His love for each of us if we are to continue to follow Him in bold trust. Too often, we move forward in faith, but we let the common and mundane issues of life weigh us down with care and discouragement. We become focused on necessary responsibilities, and forget our high calling as citizens of God's kingdom and royal children in His family.

Recently I was listening to a message by a well-known prophetic voice speaking about getting rid of yokes and receiving new mantles. As he spoke, I heard the Spirit of the

Lord say,

"I am exchanging the heavy yoke upon My people's shoulders for the mantle that carries the 'weight of My glory'."

If you are laboring with a heavy yoke and burden, now is the time to cast it off and ask for the mantle that fits you, was made for you and will rest the "weight of His glory" upon your life!

The enemy is trying to weigh many down with burdens that will distract us from intimacy and subtly entice us person into attempting to control our environment. He wants us to take matters into our own hands so that we will stop "seeking first the Kingdom of God." The enemy knows that as we seek first the Kingdom that all things will be added to us, and that is a double blow to his demonic agenda.

God is saying that this is not the time to take a heavy yoke upon yourself but to take up His light yoke and receive His mantle that will upgrade you and propel you forward with anointing and intimacy, leading to bold trust. Do not be discouraged by any challenges before you because they are fertile ground for the planting of a powerful testimony of God's faithfulness. Get excited, because if God is for you then who (or what) can stand against you?

God is sending the "weight of His glory" upon those who will ask. There is a divine exchange offered that will take the heavy yoke off your shoulders and cover you with the double portion mantle that will set you in place with anointing and the weight of His presence. This is the "Kabod" (glory, weight) which means abundance, honor, and glory!

"God, today we stand with great expectation to hear you speak, to see you move, to witness your touch, to watch you command, to experience your deliverance and to live within the power of your love!"

Day 14 Declaration

Then Jesus said, "Come to me, all of you who are weary and carry heavy burdens, and I will give you rest. Take my yoke upon you. Let me teach you, because I am humble and gentle at heart, and you will find rest for your souls. For my yoke is easy to bear, and the burden I give you is light." (Matthew 11:28-30)

Today I respond to the invitation from Jesus to exchange the weariness and the heavy yoke that has weighed me down for His rest and easy yoke. I receive the mantle that fits the call and design He created me for. I will be taught by the Lord the ways of humility and gentleness. It is with His yoke that I will become bold and courageous, for I will not be worn down or burdened, or put on and carry a yoke that does not fit me and requires my strength rather than His. I receive rest for my soul.

15

Receiving the Anointing of Purity

In these days, there is a company emerging throughout the earth: a glorious family of God's children who carry an anointing of purity. They will be a people who have yielded to the deep preparation of purification. This anointing of purity will break defilement off people, families, and nations. What they release will be like a baptism in water for the recipients as they are saturated with the purity of heaven and the washing of the Spirit. It will restore lives to the fear of the Lord and the holiness of the Lord.

There is a beauty that this purity releases which will reveal Christ in His true, pure nature; ushering in the holiness of the Lord. These people of purity will witness the glory they carry releasing the power of the blood of Jesus that washes away sin and stain.

It will be like the vision in Zechariah 3, when Joshua the high priest had his filthy garments changed by a sovereign act of God. What the Lord's family radiates will have the authority, through the anointing of purity, to rebuke the accuser and to restore sons and daughters. This will be an anointing that has the power to restore and cleanse, and display the glory of the Lord.

The anointing of purity will not come through the works of man, or his strength or his goodness, but will arrive through humility and surrender. It will be characteristic of those who have taken the posture of Mary in Luke 1:38. She was visited by the angel who announced that she would conceive a child by the power of the Holy Spirit, and she responded by saying,

"Be it unto me according to your word."

There is a deep testing that purges and strengthens these yielded ones. They will face many trials as an invitation to bow and enter deep humility and purity. They will have been refined by fire and humbled themselves at His feet in the fear of the Lord. There will be a posture of praise and the exultation of Jesus that continually brings men and women back to the place where they enthrone Him in His rightful place: over all and in all.

The anointing of purity will produce pure oil that can be received by those around them. This pure oil will be the oil that lights the lamps of the five wise virgins in Matthew 25:1-13. Each time they speak, write, create, dance, or sing they will present their lives like a white, blank canvas for the Creator of heaven and earth to paint upon as He pleases.

They will be submitted servants, teachable children, humble; transparent men and woman who are connected to the body—not living as independent islands—and who have spent many hours in the place of intercession, worship, and the study of Scripture. They will live the wisdom written in the Book of Proverbs. This is not a "suddenly" anointing; it must be paid for through preparation and sacrifice. Purity does not come apart from testing and a process. It is different than being washed clean through the forgiveness of Jesus. This "purity anointing" takes time and humility; the pure oil is dispensed through pressing.

We are now seeing these pure ones revealed and what they carry will benefit the body in ways rarely seen before this time. It is an anointing that supersedes even profound giftings. You are invited to be purified and to be a part of this company of a people of purity.

If you are going through deep testing and fiery trials, purging and preparation; know this: it is important to remain in that place! It is His love that desires to purify you so that a fresh outpouring will come to you and through you. Surrender and yield to this work. The crushing will produce pure, fresh oil that anoints you with purity.

Being yielded, surrendered, and humble will in turn cause you to walk in a bold confidence that is pure and undefiled.

Create in me a pure heart, O God. And renew a steadfast spirit within me. (Psalm 51:10)

Day 15 Declaration

Teach me your ways, O LORD, that I may live according to your truth! Grant me purity of heart, so that I may honor you. (Psalm 86:11)

Today I come and ask to be made pure as you are pure, Jesus. Create in me a pure and clean heart; a yielded, humble, and teachable heart. I declare this day that I receive the invitation to allow the process of purity to touch and transform every area of my life. I will receive your instructions and your refinement and like Mary I say, "Be it unto me according to your word." I surrender all and by an act of my will I yield to your hand and to your Spirit that makes me pure.

16

Revived Through Wisdom

One of the ways that the Lord is drawing His people out from their hiding places of timidity and insecurity into the joyous freedom of bold confidence is by sheltering them in the safety of a life guarded by His instructions. Psalm 19:7-11 says,

The instructions of the Lord are perfect, reviving the soul. The decrees of the Lord are trustworthy, making wise the simple. The commandments of the Lord are right, bringing joy to the heart. The commands of the Lord are clear, giving insight for living. Reverence for the Lord is pure, lasting forever. The laws of the Lord are true; each one is fair. They are more desirable than gold, even the finest gold. They are sweeter than honey, even honey dripping from the comb. They are a warning to your servant, a great reward for those who obey them.

The instructions of the Lord will revive your soul! Not being properly aligned with the Word of God will cause your soul to become weary and worn out. The instructions of the Lord create new and right alignments that revive every part of your soul: character, feelings, consciousness, memory, perception, and thinking. Some versions of the Bible state it this way:

The law of the Lord is perfect, converting the soul.

HIS INSTRUCTIONS PRODUCE LIFE

To enact a law is to create a system of rules that regulate actions and are enforced by the impositions of penalties. Therefore, God's law or system of rules will align your actions with His truth, and His commands are not a burden to us, but instead, when they are followed, a commanded blessing is released upon us. God's ways—His decrees, commandments, and instructions—are perfect and all-together wise. Every person ever created was "hardwired" to thrive in their body, soul, and spirit as they walk in His ways and instructions. It truly is the taste of sweet honey upon your tongue and the worth of pure gold to your soul. When you walk in His ways you receive great rewards.

The enemy is continually deceiving people into believing that if they align their lives to walk fully in God's ways that they will face personal loss or lose something important that they hold onto as their security, comfort, and treasure. Yet the very opposite is true. As you yield your life to walk in His laws or instructions your life gains many blessings, and the penalty of breaking His instructions are removed. Many live their lives focused on the things that bring temporary comfort or momentary security; yet we have been wisely counseled to store up our treasure in heaven; for there our hearts and lives will thrive.

> *"Do not store up for yourselves treasures on earth, where moths and vermin destroy, and where thieves break in and steal. But store up for yourselves treasures in heaven, where moths and vermin do not destroy, and where thieves do not break in and steal. For where your treasure is, there your heart will be also." (Matthew 6:19-21)*

Anything built from a blueprint of human ways or wisdom becomes like building your life upon sinking sand. Only what is built on the Rock of Christ will stand firm.

"Everyone then who hears these words of mine and does them will be like a wise man who built his house on the rock. And the rain fell, and the floods came, and the winds blew and beat on that house, but it did not fall, because it had been founded on the rock. And everyone who hears these words of mine and does not do them will be like a foolish man who built his house on the sand. And the rain fell, and the floods came, and the winds blew and beat against that house, and it fell, and great was the fall of it." (Matthew 7:24-27)

The Lord desires to give you an impartation of His wisdom as you put great value on His instructions. We see this in the lives of men in Scripture: Solomon asked for wisdom from the Lord; Daniel received wisdom from the Lord; and David declared the wisdom of the Lord in song and action. Your soul will receive a new boldness and confidence as you treasure the wisdom of the Lord as your instructions for living. God's wisdom brings authority, favor, and victory into your life.

The decrees of the Lord are trustworthy, making wise the simple. (Psalm 19:7)

WHAT IS WISDOM?

The wisdom of those whom the world considers wise merely makes things more convoluted and difficult to understand, but the wisdom of the Lord makes wise the simple. Likewise, religion complicates wisdom and provokes people to rely on their own works, but the true and trustworthy instructions of the Lord are bathed in the grace needed to carry them out.

The wisdom of the world says, "Hold onto your money and resources because that is your hope and security."

But the wisdom of the Lord says,

Remember this: Whoever sows sparingly will also reap sparingly, and whoever sows generously will also reap generously. Each of you should give what you have decided in your heart to give, not reluctantly or under compulsion, for God loves a cheerful giver. And God is able to bless you abundantly, so that in all things at all times, having all that you need, you will abound in every good work. (2 Corinthians 9:6-8)

The wisdom of the world says, "Your life belongs to you and you alone. Independence is strength and dependency is weakness."

But the wisdom of the Lord says,

"If you cling to your life, you will lose it, and if you let your life go, you will save it." (Luke 17:33)

His ways and instructions will revive your soul, restore your resources, make the difficult simple, give joy to your heart, and give you insight for living. His instructions have been given to revive your soul so that you can thrive in every area with bold confidence.

Day 16 Declaration

Lord, you alone are my portion and my cup; you make my lot secure.
The boundary lines have fallen for me in pleasant places; surely I have a delightful inheritance. (Psalm 16:5-6)

I declare that the instructions of the Lord are a benefit for my life. I renounce all other instructions that lead me in my own way and take up the full instruction of the Lord. His ways are the boundaries that "make my lot secure." As I walk in the instructions of the Lord and treasure His wisdom, I dwell in pleasant places and receive my delightful inheritance. His law is my delight and I choose by my freewill to receive His instructions as my counsel. You are my portion and therefore the cup that I drink from refreshes me and gives me strength, confidence, and boldness.

17

The Voice That Brings Freedom

I recently had a startling and vivid dream. I was standing in a field when a deluge of heavy rain suddenly burst from the sky; it was a downpour like I have never before witnessed—more like a flash flood erupting from heaven to earth. As the water hit the earth, flashes of lightning were accompanied by simultaneous cracks of thunder as these strikes hit a grove of tall evergreen trees, splitting them in two.

I awoke from the dream hearing the words from Psalm 29:5,

The voice of the LORD breaks the cedars; Yes, the LORD breaks in pieces the cedars of Lebanon.

The Message Bible words it like this,

God's thunder smashes cedars, God topples the northern cedars.

This dream came to me at the same time the Spirit was speaking to me daily about the need for the "fear of the Lord" to come back upon His people so they might walk boldly; releasing the fear of the Lord into the earth.

From the west, people will fear the name of the LORD, and from the rising of the sun, they will revere his glory. For he will come like a pent-up flood that the breath of the LORD drives along. (Isaiah 59:19, NIV)

The enemy seeks to flood the land through witchcraft, perversions, and evil of all sorts, but the Lord overpowers all works of darkness, because He explodes in His glory like a pent—up flood! God's voice has come and is raising up a standard! As the fear of the Lord returns to your life and to His church, it will release the awe of God that breaks—shatters—everything that has stood against Him. It anoints His people with the righteous boldness and confidence that releases the power to change culture and nations.

THE LORD'S TRUE STANDARD

"Woe unto them that call evil good, and good evil; that put darkness for light, and light for darkness; that put bitter for sweet, and sweet for bitter!" (Isaiah 5:20)

A flood of evil that is being redefined as "good" has come upon mankind that calls darkness light and light darkness. But the fear of the Lord is touching the earth with a powerful strike that brings forth the Lord's standard. You are invited to take part by inviting His voice to strike you with power and boldness.

In my dream, the trees struck by lightning were evergreen trees. Today, in the United States of America, a flag with an evergreen tree on it has become a symbol of prayer asking God to return to our nation. This flag is the "Appeal to Heaven" flag flown by George Washington's first naval ships during the War for Independence. The evergreen tree upon this flag represented "liberty" or freedom at the beginning of the beginning of the struggle. What the colonists of that day could not accomplish on earth became an appeal to heaven that achieved victory through the boldness of a few.

I was reminded of that history by my dream, and declare that now is the time to call out with your "appeal to heaven" for liberty and justice for your nation, for your children, and for your life. You can boldly approach the throne of grace today and posture your life and your requests to receive the power of His voice that gives you the breakthrough, freedom, and liberty that you need.

The definition of liberty is, "the state of being free within society from oppressive restrictions imposed by authority on one's way of life, behavior, or political views"; "the power or scope to act as one pleases."

The enemy has been rewriting his definition of liberty within the systems of the nations of the world. It has become liberty to pursue evil and call it good, while oppressing those who call for the righteous standard of God to be raised up. Within the context of the Bible the word "liberty" means freedom. This is the freedom to live apart from slavery to the masters of sin and the world's systems. In the standard of the fear of the Lord we are given freedom from the grip of slavery to sin and to unrighteousness. The enemy has set up a Babylonian culture that enslaves and blinds people from the "way of freedom" that Jesus provided for us on the cross. When Jesus died and rose again, the way was made through grace for all to be set free.

> *It is for freedom that Christ has set us free. Stand firm, then, and do not let yourselves be burdened again by a yoke of slavery. (Galatians 5:1)*

GRACE THAT OPEN THE FLOODGATES

When Jesus died, the veil in the Temple in Jerusalem that barred entrance into the presence of God was torn, and we were given free access to boldly come before the throne of grace so that we could be reconciled with God, enjoying His presence always, where true liberty is found. I believe the nations of this world are about to see a great "rending of the veil" that has blinded the eyes of the world from seeing their Messiah. The gods of this world have stood like trees, creating a veil that blinds people from seeing Jesus and from the revelation of true liberty and freedom. These "gods" have cast a shadow of darkness that perverts the truth, calling darkness light and light darkness.

But wait! The Lord has the final say! His voice thunders, breaking the cedars and rending the veil of separation between God and man. As the Lord returns the awe and the fear of the Lord to His church it is releasing a flood and a sound that lifts up His presence and glory, sweeping away evil with a tsunami of righteousness and truth.

> *"The time will come," says the LORD, "when the grain and grapes will grow faster than they can be harvested. Then the terraced vineyards on the hills of Israel will drip with sweet wine!" (Amos 9:13)*

Once again you can invite the fear of the Lord to come upon your life, your family, your church, your city, and your nation. You are a part of the whole body and as the corporate anointing is established in the fear of the Lord, it will bring liberty and freedom to both the individual and the whole.

Day Seventeen Declaration

So let us keep on coming boldly to the throne of grace, so that we may obtain mercy and find grace to help us in our time of need. (Hebrews 4:16)

Today I receive the voice of the Lord upon my life. His voice breaks the cedars and His voice is the voice of boldness within me. I declare that I will not remain silent as the enemy seeks to release a false narrative over my life, my children, or my nation. I call darkness dark and that which is unrighteous I call evil; but I declare that the ways of the Lord are good, righteous, and full of light.

I declare the true liberty and freedom that comes from Christ over my life. I am not a slave to fear but I am set free and given liberty as I live in the fear of the Lord. My silence is now exchanged for bold confidence and I will boldly go to the throne of grace to obtain mercy and find grace that will help me when I am in need. I will not stand back in timidity or as an orphan, but I approach Him as a son or daughter who has been given full rights to approach Him day or night.

18

God Will Do What You Cannot

One day as I was waiting on the Lord, He showed me people lying in bed, their minds flooded with anxious thoughts that led them to conclusions of dread and doom for the days ahead. But the Father came to comfort them saying,

"Do not fear, do not worry, and do not dread the days ahead for I will do for you what you cannot do for yourself. You can trust me."

As the people responded in confident trust, the gripping fear was washed away and peace restored them to rest in His promises.

Are there times that you are being driven by fear and anxious thoughts? If so, the Lord wants you to hear His words of truth and words of hope. He is not unaware of the things that you have gone through or the insecurities about what you might be facing. He will do for you what you cannot do for yourself.

Sleepless nights caused by anxious thoughts and fears will often lead your thoughts down dead-end roads with hopeless prospects. The Lord will come in those anxious nights to exchange the "dread ahead" for a deep and peaceful sleep like that of a baby in its mother's arms. He will usher you into His green pastures and lead you beside the still waters that bring you into hope and confidence in His plans for you.

"For I know the plans I have for you," declares the Lord, "plans to prosper you and not to harm you, plans to give you hope and a future." (Jeremiah 29:11)

You will lie down in peace and wake up in joy because you can be confident that the Lord has taken up your cause! Even in those times that you find yourself caught in a tangled net, you can be confident that the Lord will rescue you. Though at times you don't feel adequate or able to find your way out of the circumstances that you find yourself in, know that He is able to rescue you!

Such is the confidence and steadfast reliance and absolute trust that we have through Christ toward God. Not that we are sufficiently qualified in ourselves to claim anything as coming from us, but our sufficiency and qualifications come from God. (2 Corinthians 3:4-5, AMP)

Christ qualifies you for success, for breakthrough, and for a positive outcome. It is in yielding your life to "steadfast reliance and absolute trust…through Christ toward God" that your confidence is restored and you are saved and protected and able to move forward with boldness. You will be secure and steadfast because you know you are in His care.

Have you ever seen a wild deer caught in barbed wire fencing? It will flail in fear in its frantic efforts to escape, only to find itself held tighter in the snare's grip. When help comes to free the deer, the rescuers must hold it still in order to release it and keep it from greater harm. The Lord will hold you still and cut away the barbs and snares that trap and pierce you. Do not fear, for He is with you and He will always free you from the tangled snares that you find yourself caught in. He will do for you what you cannot do for yourself!

Be calm, be still, and watch to see the salvation of the Lord on your behalf.

Bu Moses told the people "Don't be afraid. Just stand still and watch the LORD rescue you today. The Egyptians you see today will never be seen again. The LORD himself will fight for you. Just stay calm." (Exodus 14:13-14)

Day Eighteen Declaration

Don't fret or worry. Instead of worrying, pray. Let petitions and praises shape your worries into prayers, letting God know your concerns. Before you know it, a sense of God's wholeness, everything coming together for good, will come and settle you down. It's wonderful what happens when Christ displaces worry at the center of your life. Philippians 4:6-7

I declare that from this day forward I will not allow my days and nights to be consumed by anxious thoughts and fears. When those thoughts and emotions come upon me, as they most assuredly will, I will ask God to take every thought captive and invite His peace to guard my heart and mind with the faithfulness of Christ. I know that God works everything together for my good and that He is the one who rescues me when I cry to Him for help. I will be still and rest in the knowledge that He is God and He is good.

I displace worry with bold confidence in my Father's love for me and His desire to help me even when I cannot help myself. Thank you, Jesus, for being my hope and my deliverer.

19

Wrestle Until God Wins

There are seasons in our lives when we enter a time of "wrestle" between our soul and what the Spirit is desiring to do within us. Many feelings may accompany this time of wrestling, but be assured that the wrestle is worth the reward! It may cause pain–it may even cause confusion–but as you wrestle down the defenses in your soul that have become barriers to the deeper experience of oneness with Christ, it will be the best fight you will ever lose!

As Christ is forged and formed in you, He will overthrow other things have occupied you, taking up space within your heart and mind. Often these things are so familiar and comforting that they cause blind spots in our lives, until circumstances crash us against the shores of false beliefs. We often don't see the dark places that the enemy has been occupying until we enter the wrestle to see Jesus formed in us. The enemy does not want greater surrender or refinement in our lives because he knows that the more we yield to Jesus, the more light we will reveal that dispels darkness.

The Spirit of the Lord is preparing His people by occupying greater amounts of territory in their lives. This requires us to war against strongholds that the enemy has held within us. To wrestle these places down we must face the fears that have fortified these strongholds. We must boldly battle down false securities, idols, and comforts that we've carried like a child's security blanket. He will ask to leave behind childish things so that the enemy will no longer have a place in us.

The ways of the Holy One are upside-down and backwards to the ways of man or the ways of human reasoning. Therefore when we begin to enter the ways of God, we can experience a type of spiritual and emotional vertigo. This vertigo can cause us to try to regain balance through old or familiar ways and by relying on strongholds that have caused us to feel in control. It is vital that we get still in order to allow the Spirit to reorient us to the atmosphere of His glorious Kingdom and His beautiful character.

This is of wrestle is not a time to back down or to run ahead, but rather to wrestle down the "flight" mode of the discomforts that accompany change and transformation. This is a time of fight, not flight. Fight for stillness, fight for surrender, fight for yieldedness, and fight against everything that is in your soul that is preventing you from seeing Christ formed in you!

Day Nineteen Declaration

To them God has chosen to make known among the Gentiles the glorious riches of this mystery, which is Christ in you, the hope of glory. He is the one we proclaim, admonishing and teaching everyone with all wisdom, so that we may present everyone fully mature in Christ. To this end I strenuously contend with all the energy Christ so powerfully works in me. (Colossians 1:27-29)

I will not run away from the work of the Spirit that desires to see Christ formed within me. I declare to my soul that I will surrender to His Spirit even when my emotions and my thoughts betray me. I will allow His Word and His ways to be formed within me and I will wrestle until Christ wins and until I come into a oneness with my God. I will leave behind old familiar ways that have kept me from seeing His character formed in me; even ways that have comforted me by giving me a sense of control. I surrender control to the wisdom of His Spirit.

Search me Lord! Find the ways, beliefs, and places that keep my life ruled by me rather than you. I will boldly pray for you to win so that I will be found fully yours.

20

Boldly Say Yes

Our family recently experienced a suddenly—an exciting one—when during the same week, two of our sons (one in New York and one in California), separately heard the Lord speak to them that it was time to move to where we live in Oregon to be a part of our ministry and church family. Neither of our sons spoke to the other about this, but they both shared it with my husband and me. They spent a few months waiting for some sort of sure confirmation before acting on what they felt they heard from God. As each young man waited for a sign of confirmation before committing themselves, both of them became frustrated and confused because nothing seemed to happen; it was as if they were stalled, unable to move forward.

Then the Spirit spoke to each of them separately and said, *"Your yes is what is needed."*

Within a few days of each other, they both said "yes" to the Lord in faith, trusting His word spoken into their hearts. As soon as they did, doors began to open, circumstances shifted, and miracles of provision occurred. It was an exciting and faith-building time for all of us.

Often, we put greater confidence in a sign or a confirmation than we do in the still, small voice that His sheep know. We can go forward in bold confidence at the sound of His voice. Though there is nothing wrong with seeking confirmation and counsel, there are times that our confirmation comes with the response to His voice.

OUR "YES" IS THE KEY

Throughout my life, God has asked my husband and me to do things that had such crazy risk attached to them that people who did not understand faith questioned our sanity. We've said yes to leaving our home and moving to other states and other countries with nothing but the word of the Lord. Our yes became the beginning of the shaking of the ground that crumbled the mountains that stood before us like impossible obstacles. Our yes became a rod in our hand like the rod of Moses that parted the Red Sea before the Israelites. Our yes became the bold response that was needed to advance forward.

Has the Lord ever asked you to do something that appears impossible? Does your bold yes make you appear crazy to those who are looking on, and maybe crazy to you as well? You are in good company! Noah surely looked crazy as he built a boat the size of a ship where there was no water. But He heard the voice of His God. Noah's yes saved His family and spared God's amazing animals. His yes would have saved other people if they had been willing to listen to the word of the Lord through Noah. God's servant had to step out in faith during the years it took to build the Ark, and his confirmation was the rain that did not come until he had finished.

The testimony of Jesus is the spirit of prophecy. Allow Noah's testimony and Moses' testimony to serve as prophetic illustrations over your life. Recount the faithfulness of God that is recorded in His Word and in your life, speaking His goodness aloud to your children and your children's children. The stories you tell will impart boldness and confidence to your family, encouraging them in their own journey of learning to follow the Lord's instructions and requests.

Say yes! Bold obedience to His voice is the key to the door that stands before you. Waiting for the door to open before allowing your key of "yes" to be inserted will only delay you from entering into greater encounters of promise and provision. Your "yes" will be the release of everything that you need. As you step forward, each step will release the provision, grace, and strength for what you need. Let the "fear of the Lord" become greater than the fear of the unknown. He is faithful and He has gone before you.

> *And the peace of God, which transcends all understanding, will guard your hearts and your minds in Christ Jesus. (Philippians 4:7)*

Day 20 Declaration

...you must commit yourselves wholeheartedly to these commands that I am giving you today. Impress them on your children. Talk about them when you sit at home and when you walk along the road, when you lie down and when you get up. Tie them as symbols on your hands and bind them on your foreheads. Write them on the doorframes of your houses and on your gates. (Deuteronomy 6:6-9)

Today I declare that I will trust in your voice with bold confidence. I will no longer accept any lie that tells me I do not hear the voice of my God, because your Word makes it clear that your sheep know your voice. I will be bold with my "yes" to every request you make of me. I will recount the stories of old as the testimony of Jesus and the spirit of prophesy. I will speak them, remember them, and meditate on them day and night. I declare that my "yes" is like the rod of Moses and the ark that saved Noah and his family. I do not need to understand but rather I will trust and obey. Even now I declare YES to your will and your requests. I put my confidence in God alone and from that posture I can walk in boldness.

21

Bold Obedience!

We are living in a time where the Lord is raising up a people who will listen for His voice of wisdom and instruction and then they will boldly and fearlessly obey. These will be a people who will not be dictated to by circumstances, who will not delay following God's leading because they don't "see" a physical manifestation of the resources they need, but instead they will hear and obey, and then they will see God move!

God has always had people He called to be pioneers. My husband and I have walked in this type of lifestyle for the past twenty years on behalf of our family (and His family), and now we are seeing our children walk in this way. Faith is not what we can see; if it were, it would not be faith. Faith is in the unseen promise, yet it is our assurance of things promised and hoped for.

When the Lord speaks, He is extending an invitation to respond. As we add our "yes" it becomes our agreement and partnership with His invitation. As we obey, we begin to see God move. Of course we need to seek His timing, but in my experience, He is always faithful to reveal that to us. Delaying our "yes" based on some need to see provision first is not fully responding to His invitation. Your "yes" attaches your life to the provision of heaven.

Our family has watched the miraculous and amazing

provision of the Lord time and time again as we said yes to decisions that seemed ridiculous and impossible in the natural; but we had "heavenly assurance" because God spoke, we obeyed in faith, and then He moved.

> *"Whether you turn to the right or to the left, your ears will hear a voice behind you, saying, 'This is the way; walk in it.'" Isaiah 30:21*

Make a practice of listening and it will open your spiritual ears to hear clearly! As you hear be sure to obey and watch how your faith and confidence grows. This will prepare you to hear and obey things that exceed your wildest dreams.

I often hear people question why God doesn't use them to do the "greater works." May I suggest that He uses those who have made it their lifestyle to listen and obey? I believe He has amazing plans for every one of His people. The key to living in those plans is to walk in them; it is truly the "road less traveled." The path of living "reasonably" or "practically" usually leads to the ordinary, but the path of supernatural living leads to the extraordinary. Bold trust in God leads to bold obedience which will cause you to walk in bold, greater works.

One of the hallmarks of the season we have entered is convergence. There have been many prophetic words released about "time"; words like, "The Time is Now," "A Marker in Time," "Now is the Time," "It's Time!" I have been in many conversations with other prophetic voices who are hearing clocks, bells, whistles, alarms, and words that go back many years becoming NOW words.

We are in a convergence of time: time past and a now or kairos time; the old and new; the past and present all colliding into a NOW time. One time, one people, one family, ONE God!

I saw a vision of men, women, and children all walking in different places around the world, all in different time zones and doing different activities. But suddenly each person's watch synchronized and reset to the same time and alarms went off simultaneously. There were pocket watches that older men carried, wrist watches that the middle-aged people were wearing, and smart watches worn by the younger generation. They all synchronized and as they did one family emerged; three generations walking as one with one God!

When I looked at the different watches to see the time, I began to see many times overlaid as one kairos time. I saw 10:10, 11:11, 12:12…but they were somehow all a "now time."

Then verses began to flood through my mind. Verses such as these:

"The thief comes only to steal and kill and destroy; I have come that they may have life, and have it to the full." John 10:10

"And by faith even Sarah, who was past childbearing age, was enabled to bear children because she considered him faithful who had made the promise." Hebrews 11:11

"For the Holy Spirit will teach you at that time what you should say." Luke 12:12

I began to hear to hear prophetic words that were brought to my remembrance from the 80s, 90s, and early 2000s. Then I heard words from our present day and they all converged into one sound that signaled the family to emerge and converge.

I am sure that what I experienced was limited to my understanding and that there was so much more happening than I was aware of, because I could hear echoes of years gone by and prayers for tomorrow as if they were one sound. It sounded like the worship in Revelation 4:11 before the throne that caused the elders to cast down their crowns and cry out,

"You are worthy, our Lord and God, to receive glory and honor and power, for you created all things, and by your will they were created and have their being."

Then the words, "Holy, holy, holy" rang out and the men,

women, and children now on earth joined with heaven, casting down their crowns. Suddenly men's hearts were purified, and a remnant was made ready for a move of God that would be marked by purity and oneness.

The time is now. The convergence of time is upon us and the sound of heaven and earth is aligned to give Him all the glory He deserves.

The Lord's written Word and spoken word need to be heard and practiced. Jesus is the door and He is the Word; therefore when we put His words into action it becomes a doorway to living in an abundant life. You can trust Him! He is faithful to all His promises. When the Lord asks something of you there is always a guarantee and promise attached to it. He does not ask and then leave you without provision. It may not always look like you'd expect, but it will come in a way that will have His "fingerprints" all over it. You can trust His continual guidance and correction as you step out courageously in the boldness that is produced by obedience.

Day 21 Declaration

Believe me when I say that I am in the Father and the Father is in me; or at least believe on the evidence of the works themselves. Very truly I tell you, whoever believes in me will do the works I have been doing, and they will do even greater things than these, because I am going to the Father. And I will do whatever you ask in my name, so that the Father may be glorified in the Son. You may ask me for anything in my name, and I will do it. (John 14:11-14)

I declare this day that I will walk in bold obedience. I will not wait to say yes to what you ask of me based on circumstances or proof, but in faith and trust I will give you my "yes" at the time that you ask. I turn away from withholding my obedience due to fear but now I put my faith in you knowing that you do not ask anything of me that you do not provide for me. The time is now, you are doing new things and I will be part of them, remembering that nothing is impossible for you.

22

Going Deeper

God has placed an insatiable thirst in the lives of His people that causes them to run after Him with desperate abandonment. Our desire grows and our thirst is like a man stumbling on a desert road, scorched by the noonday sun, throat parched and tongue swollen by desperate thirst. That man will go to any lengths to get a drink, and when he finally finds water he will drink deeply. Thirsting after God is a gift because it causes us to search for Him like a desperate man in search of refreshment. There are times it seems the water that we so desperately desire evades our reach. But it is in those times that our capacity for drinking deeply is expanded and stretched in the depths of our souls.

In Luke 5 we find Simon frustrated from a long night of fishing with no results. He is tired and empty-handed, and though it does not say he was desperate, one can imagine the desperation he felt after having no results; no pay-off for all his work. In verse 4 Jesus addresses Simon saying,

> *"Put out into the deep water and let down your nets for a catch."*

Desperation will cause us to do what we wouldn't do if we had received what we wanted in our first attempt. Simon responded to the Lord's request and went out again into the lake. He threw his nets into deep waters and found more fish than he could ask or imagine when he pulled in his nets.

In my life, there have been many times when I felt as though I worked through a long night season only to come up short, and it is in those times that I have heard the Lord speak similar words to me, *"Daughter, go deeper. Throw yourselves into the depths of My love and watch what you draw in."*

Then, like Simon, who fell on his knees before the Lord, I find myself in a new awareness of how great His love is toward me and I fall on my knees before Him once again. When I again drink deeply of His love, I begin to experience the manifestation of Psalm 42:7,

> *"Deep calls to deep at the sound of Your waterfalls; All Your breakers and Your waves have rolled over me."*

And again, my heart finds courage and I am given renewed boldness to run after Him, knowing that with every step I am drawn into greater depths, and I cry out like Romans 11:33:

> *"Oh, the depth of the riches both of the wisdom and knowledge of God! How unsearchable are His judgments and unfathomable His ways!"*

Hunger and thirst are gifts. Desperation and pain are gifts. Longing and waiting are gifts. Even hope deferred can be a gift, because in the delay, we are invited into deep places and can experience the unsearchable and unfathomable ways of His love. Desire fulfilled is far more beautiful to the desperately thirsty soul than it is to the satisfied soul. He is calling you deeper, deeper, and deeper still. Let Him draw you into the deep waters where you will find a love beyond comprehension.

Day 22 Declaration

And I pray that you, being rooted and established in love, may have power, together with all the Lord's holy people, to grasp how wide and long and high and deep is the love of Christ, and to know this love that surpasses knowledge—that you may be filled to the measure of all the fullness of God. (Ephesians 3:17-19)

I declare over my life that I will thirst after God like a "deer pants for water" (Psalm 42). I will not stop or give up until I find the depths of your love out of the deep waters of your presence. My life will be rooted and established in the depths and width of your love. I will allow my hunger, my pain, my longings, and my disappointments to usher me into surpassing knowledge of who you are. Today is a day that I ask you to begin to take me into experiences of the depths of your love and to be established in the fullness of God.

23

You Are Not A Survivor; You Are an Over-comer!

God has not called us to survive this world but to overcome the world. Simply "hanging on" does not lead to confidence, courage, or boldness; but rather, such a posture leads to fear, defensiveness, and insecurities. I often hear people declare that they are a survivor and though that is not a negative thing, God calls us to more than mere survival; He calls us to overcome. Victims of a horrific event may still be alive, but that doesn't mean that they have overcome the trauma and pain. A survivor is generally associated with trauma, whereas the over-comer is connected to victory.

In an earlier chapter, I wrote of the time I experienced my "dark night of the soul." I was a young wife and mother functioning in ministry, and I struggled through a three-year time period that was a pivotal time for me to move from survivor to overcomer. I had survived years of intense difficulty, but I was not aware that I still needed to enter the victory that Jesus had provided to overcome the effects my past had on my life. I took survival skills into my marriage, my parenting, and ministry. Though these skills caused my daily life to appear fine outwardly, unresolved issues were tearing me up on the inside.

I finally felt the Lord asking me to allow Him to deal with

this survival mentality that had become so familiar to me. The first couple of years consisted of me using survival skills to spiritually overcome—using what I felt I knew—rather than humbly surrender to the Spirit's work in my life. That merely caused all the hidden pain to surface without the power and authority to overcome. I spiraled down into a deep and dark depression as my "skills" fell alarmingly short of controlling the unbearable pain I was experiencing. I did not realize during that time that at the root of all the pain and trauma was a spirit of death that had entered my life at an early age. Only through the overcoming power of Christ over death was I going to be free.

When the spirit of death was made clear to me, I entered the battle of all battles. This wicked spirit did not want to let go without taking my life. I had to learn the beauty of surrender and of coming into a full dependency upon the Holy Spirit in order to appropriate Jesus' victory over death and the grave. One particular day—after a very close brush with death—this battle came to a head. I found myself on the threshold between life and death. I needed to choose; "survival" was no longer an option. I was forced to decide if I would receive life by submitting to the Lord and letting Him remove the spirit of death, or continuing the path I was on and lose my life. After the most intense hour of my life, where I truly faced a "showdown" between life and death, I humbled myself and let go of the last vestiges of control and surrendered to His overcoming victory. In that moment, the spirit of death was defeated, and life was restored. I fully put my trust in God; I put my faith in Him and His overcoming victory. I chose life and let go of the spirit of death that was demanding so much from me.

In the following weeks and months, I experienced courage and boldness that I had never known before. I moved from being in the grip of surviving the thief—who comes to steal, kill and destroy (John 10:10)—to life and life abundantly! No longer was I surviving or relying upon survival skills to hold things together but now I was daily experiencing the beauty and power of the victorious life.

If you find yourself in some sort of battle for survival, then take heart and realize that there is life beyond survival! Our Lord overcame the world; He overcame for my sake and yours. What He paid for He has freely given to us, His beloved ones. No matter what you are facing or what you are feeling, God has a message for you:

"You will overcome!" You will overcome by the blood of the Lamb and the word of your testimony!

> *They triumphed over him by the blood of the Lamb and by the word of their testimony; they did not love their lives so much as to shrink from death. Revelation 12:11*

It is time to apply the blood of the Lamb upon the doorpost of your life, just as Israel did the night of Passover in Egypt. The blood of the Lamb who was slain will cause the power of death to pass by you and not be able to touch you. Declare the victory of Jesus upon your head and on your loved ones. Declare that the precious blood of Jesus covers every shortcoming, every sin, every disappointment, and releases every victory.

It is time to release the sounds of your testimony. The words and remembrances of His faithfulness are like a sharpened double-edged sword that cuts through everything that has stood against you.

GREAT IS HIS FAITHFULNESS!

As you begin to recount the testimonies of His faithfulness in your life and speak them out, even if no one is listening, it will change the atmosphere around you. You will receive another testimony of His goodness and mercy because you will be prophesying the testimony of Jesus back over your life. You will see the vast sea that has stood before you part and your enemy swallowed up as you pass over on dry land. You will witness the greatness of our God and then testify to all who will listen.

The sound of your testimony and His faithfulness going forth will be like ripples in water that will build the overcoming spirit in you; every mountain that has hindered you or caused you to lose courage will be removed. It is time to recall His faithfulness and goodness to your friends and your family; and even into the atmosphere when you are alone. It will not come back void!

As I hear the Lord declaring the words, "You will overcome," I also hear a resounding response from His people that says, "GREAT IS YOUR FAITHFULNESS!"

The faithful love of the Lord never ends! His mercies never cease. Great is his faithfulness; his mercies begin afresh each morning. I say to myself, "The Lord is my inheritance; therefore, I will hope in him!"
(Lamentations

Let His promise of overcoming wash over you like a refreshing waterfall of love. He will not disappoint you.

Revelation 12:11 They triumphed over him by the blood of the Lamb and by the word of their testimony; they did not love their lives so much as to shrink from death. (Revelation 12:11)

For everyone born of God overcomes the world. This is the victory that has overcome the world, even our faith. (1 John 5:4)

This day I call the heavens and the earth as witnesses against you that I have set before you life and death, blessings and curses. Now choose life, so that you and your children may live 20 and that you may love the Lord your God, listen to his voice, and hold fast to him. For the Lord is your life, and he will give you many years in the land he swore to give to your fathers, Abraham, Isaac and Jacob.(Deuteronomy 30:19-20)

Day 23 Declaration

With God and His heavenly hosts as my witnesses, today I choose life! I choose blessings and the prosperity of my soul. I will no longer survive this life, but I will live in the abundance that you paid for when you gave up your life for me. I reject death and all that is associated with sin and death. I remove every place of trusting in myself or in human strength to move forward. I surrender fully to trust in you and put my faith in you to overcome my world, because you have overcome the world.

I declare the blood of the Lamb, Jesus Christ, upon my life and over the doorpost of my life, my family, and my home. His blood has given me a triumphant victory and has removed the sting of death. Therefore, I will not shrink back in fear, but I will stand firm in boldness and courage knowing that my life is built upon the foundation of His unshakable faithfulness. I will remind my soul of His faithful acts of old and I will recount them before men and into the atmosphere around me, knowing that there is power in the testimony of Jesus Christ. I declare before heaven and earth: "Great is His faithfulness!"

24

Your 10:10 Turnaround

During a time of prayer, I saw a vision of the numbers 10:10. Suddenly, the numbers switched, reversing position and revealing a "new" 10:10. Then the Lord said,

"My abundant life is overtaking and arresting the thief that came in to kill, steal, and destroy from my sons and daughters."

God is intent in this season to ensure that His plan and purpose for His people is overtaking the thief's purposes; those fears and unbelief and failures that have robbed many of God's people from experiencing a rich and abundant life.

> "The thief's purpose is to steal and kill and destroy. My purpose is to give them a rich and satisfying (abundant) life." (John 10:10)

The Lord continues to dismantle fear so that He can restore to you a spirit of bold confidence in Him. Partnering with fear unlocks and opens the back door that the enemy (the thief) comes through. As you continue to exchange a spirit of fear for the fear of the Lord, which encompasses His perfect love that casts out fear, it is evicting the thief from your life and closing the avenues he has come through. Satan is a deceiver and liar; he does not enter through the front gate, but always works in shadows and whispers to distort truth and discourage the body of Christ. Too often, as the enemy attempts to mimic the voice of God, we allow ourselves to indulge the lies because they contain a small element of "truth." But the reality is, our good Shepherd's voice always bring strength and comfort, even in correction. The voice of the enemy is harsh and grating, leaving us feeling empty and hopeless. But the voice of our Lord is powerful and uplifting, and the fear of the Lord is clean, refreshing our souls with His purity.

In John 10:7-9, we read Jesus' promise to us,

> "...I tell you the truth, I am the gate for the sheep. All who came before me were thieves and robbers. But the true sheep did not listen to them. Yes, I am the gate. Those who come in through me will be saved. They will come and go freely and will find good pastures."

THE DOOR INTO LIFE ABUNDANT

Jesus is our entrance into the goodness He offers, and as you allow Him to be the only doorway in your life then you will experience green pastures and a safe dwelling place where the thief cannot enter. The foundation of the fear of the Lord is the doorway to many promises. It becomes your divine turn-around of John 10:10!

> "You prepare a table before me in the presence of my enemies. You have anointed and refreshed my head with oil; My cup overflows. Surely goodness and mercy and unfailing love shall follow me all the days of my life, And I shall dwell forever [throughout all my days] in the house and in the presence of the LORD." (Psalm 23:5-6)

The thief may be present and roaming about this world, but even in the presence of our enemies who might wish to devour us, God prepares for us a feast of His goodness and unfailing love. Jesus is the entrance gate to this place and the thief cannot and dares not pass through.

So, you can claim the Lord's turnaround to protect you and evict the thief from your life; the lying criminal that climbs over the back wall of the sheep pen by way of unholy fear. The fear of the Lord, which fully encompasses His perfect and unfailing love, is restoring you to the place of living in the fullness of Psalm 23.

> *The Lord is my shepherd, I lack nothing.*
> *He makes me lie down in green pastures,*
> *he leads me beside quiet waters, he refreshes my soul.*
> *He guides me along the right paths for his name's sake.*
> *Even though I walk through the darkest valley, I will fear no evil,*
> *for you are with me;*
> *your rod and your staff, they comfort me.*
> *You prepare a table before me in the presence of my enemies.*
> *You anoint my head with oil; my cup overflows.*
> *Surely your goodness and love will follow me*
> *all the days of my life,*
> *and I will dwell in the house of the Lord forever.*

This is a holy shift that is resetting your life and restoring promises and inheritances that were stolen from you. Today you can enter this "10:10 Turnaround" and this shift that releases rich, satisfying, and abundant life to you. Bring your faith as an offering and place it under the safety of the fear of the Lord. Declare a fast from every other fear that has robbed you from living in abundant life.

Day 24 Declaration

Therefore Jesus said again, "Very truly I tell you, I am the gate for the sheep. All who have come before me are thieves and robbers, but the sheep have not listened to them. I am the gate; whoever enters through me will be saved. They will come in and go out, and find pasture. The thief comes only to steal and kill and destroy; I have come that they may have life, and have it to the full.(John 10:7-10)

Today I go through the gate of Jesus Christ into the promise of green pastures and still waters that He has opened before me. I declare that I have entered the shift that evicts the thief and restores to me all that has been stolen from my life through partnership with fear. I will have life and have it "to the full" because Christ died to give me abundant and eternal life. I will sit down at the table that the Lord has set for me and feast upon His goodness and unfailing love. Though my enemies are present, and though they wish to rage against me, they cannot come through the gate that I entered, therefore they cannot touch me. I will fear no evil for you, Lord, are with me and my trust is in you alone. My only fear is the fear of the Lord which makes me bold and strong.

25

The Path that Overflows

There is a pathway that all believers are invited to journey on throughout their lives. It is a path less traveled and a path unknown by those who do not know Christ. It's a path that doesn't make sense to our human reason and a path that cannot be planned out through natural understanding. This path that we are invited to journey on merely requires surrender and dependency. It requires that you surrender the demand to understand, surrender the dependency you have on walking by your sight, and it requires you to lay down your independence. It is called the path of hope and trust.

As you let go of your ways and ask the Spirit to set you on the path that follows His leading alone, only then will you discover true joy and peace.

> *May the God of hope fill you with all joy and peace as you trust in him, so that you may overflow with hope by the power of the Holy Spirit. (Romans 15:13)*

I once heard the Spirit say to me, *"Do not settle for a glass half full when you can have one that overflows."* I have found that as I follow the leading of the Holy Spirit my cup overflows. His path throws the plans of the enemy into absolute confusion. The devil doesn't understand the movements or ways of the Spirit. Just as God's ways confound and confuse our human minds, they confound and confuse the enemy. Even when following Him doesn't seem easy, He always leads us in paths of righteousness and life. The safest avenue you will ever walk is this path of hope and trust in God alone. It's not only a shortcut with less bumps and obstacles but it's also the only one that promises the benefits of joy and peace.

WORDS OF LIFE IN AN AIRPLANE

Recently, I had an encounter that caused me to once again marvel at the way the Holy Spirit orchestrates events to fulfill His purposes, even when we don't realize what is happening. I was traveling with my daughter, Amy, to take part in a ministry venture on the other side of the county. We were flying on an airline that does not give reserve seating; your place in line for boarding is determined by how early you check in for your flight.

When I fly with this company, I always pre-check twenty-four-hours ahead so I can be in the first boarding group, but somehow for this trip I completely forgot until a few hours before the flight. So, Amy and I were both put into the last group to board, which meant we wouldn't sit together and we'd both get middle seats. Honestly, I was a bit frustrated at my forgetfulness; I had been thinking about pre-check the night before and it is something I simply do not forget to do.

When it was time for our group to board, the counter person announced that the plane was full and directed us to take the first seats we found available. I walked onto the plane and set my purse on the first seat available; then I realized there wasn't any room in the overhead bin for my carry-on. Leaving my purse on my seat, I went further down the aisle to find an available compartment. After storing my case about ten rows back from my seat, a flight attendant asked if I could take a seat near where I was. I agreed and began to sit next to a man, but she said, "No, not there." I looked on the other side and saw two women talking; one was in the aisle seat and the other sat by the window, so I asked if I could sit between them. They agreed, even though they were obviously traveling together.

Amy retrieved my purse for me and returned to her seat near the front of the plane. As she walked away, I immediately thought, "God moved me for a reason." So, I began to listen.

About thirty minutes into the flight I looked at the lady near the window and heard the Lord say, "Tell her that daughter will be okay." Then I asked the Lord if He had more to say and I heard, "Ask her if her daughter's middle name is Rose because she will fully blossom and fulfill her purpose in life." The woman was wearing headphones, and I didn't want to interrupt, her so I waited a while before saying anything.

Finally, I just excused myself and asked to speak to her. When I told her that the Lord spoke to me and said her daughter would be okay, her eyes filled with tears and she said, "My sixteen-year-old daughter was diagnosed with cancer in November."

This mom was far more scared than her daughter. She told me her daughter was incredible and brave, but the lady was struggling as she watched her daughter going through chemotherapy and losing her beautiful hair. Her daughter, at age four, had started donating her hair to "Locks of Love," a charity that makes wigs for children with cancer who have lost their hair. Every year her daughter would grow her hair out and then have it cut to donate to this organization. The girl even got her community and peers involved in joining her. Now she was the one with cancer, and was losing all her hair.

I then asked the lady if her daughter's middle name was Rose. I honestly doubted my "hearing" about this, because it is not a common name these days for a sixteen-year-old. I told her that the Lord showed me that Rose would fully bloom. Her eyes wide, the lady answered, "Yes! When I was pregnant with her, I saw her as a beautiful rose that would bloom over time, so I named her Elizabeth Rose."

There was more conversation, but this mother's heart was put at ease that her daughter would be okay, and God confirmed it with a deeply personal "rose." She said she already believed in God and believed that God was the one who inspired the name Rose, but I could see how this very tender word was taking her belief to a new level and revealing His love in a very tangible way.

Encounters like this remind us how God orders and establishes our steps. He orchestrated every detail to assure that I would sit in that very seat because a mom's heart needed comforting assurance. I'm so grateful that I didn't give into frustration, or in doubt hold back the part about her daughter's middle name being Rose, because that detail was the Lord's signature upon the word that made it unmistakable to this lady. I could have remained frustrated about my forgetfulness, about losing my seat, at the crowded plane, and for not being near my daughter, but the Holy Spirit has taught me that He has my steps—and my seats—planned ahead of time.

Pay attention when something disrupts your schedule or your plans, because God may be setting you up to be His mouthpiece. He is a good, good Father!

In my life I rarely know where I'm going; I often can't perceive the details of how provision will come or how I will accomplish something God has called me to, or what will happen as I follow His leading. But what I do know is that there has been more of an overflow of fruitfulness, wisdom, and provision as I have followed His path then there ever was when I walked in my own understanding. Joy and peace accompany me like faithful companions all along the way. Every day is like walking in the company of those who have a surprise for you. Joy and peace lead me with such enthusiasm and confidence that it becomes contagious.

It's never too late to begin your journey on this path less traveled—the path that overflows with hope, joy, and great expectations. Let go and let God!

Day 25 Declaration

"Commit your way to the Lord; trust in him and he will do this: He will make your righteous reward shine like the dawn, your vindication like the noonday sun." Psalm 37:5

"The steps of a man are established by the Lord, when he delights in his way..." Psalm 37:23

Though I make my plans according to the best of my understanding and wisdom, I declare that today I commit all of those plans to you, God. You have my permission to order and establish my steps according to your ways and your will. When things aren't going how I planned or expected I will stop and listen to determine if you are re-ordering my steps according to your purposes. I declare this day that I will walk the path less traveled, the path that is determined, ordered, and established by the leading of your Spirit. I surrender my plans for your will. I surrender my rights for your ways. I become more aware of how you are ordering my steps and I surrender my path for the steps of the Lord.

26

It's Time for Crazy Courage!

I had a dream that I was walking through a house with my husband, my youngest daughter, and her husband. I immediately became aware that this house had a demon living in it. As we walked through the various hallways in the house, I felt a pervading sense of fear and dark wickedness, which increased moment by moment. We ventured up to the second floor, and from the head of the stairs, I looked down a hallway and saw a room with a closed door. Somehow, I knew that the demon was in that room. I asked my family members to stay in the hallway and wait for me. I strode to the door and pushed it open and was instantly enveloped with an appalling fear that congealed the atmosphere like a tangible presence. I took a breath and walked in and closed the door.

I glanced around the dingy surroundings and noticed that the only item in the room was a plush velvet rocking chair with a blanket draped over it. The room had one window covered with velveteen drapes. I went to the chair and sat down, hoping that if I were comfortable, I could better handle the fear that permeated the room. As I settled into the chair, I felt my fear intensify, so I tugged the blanket from the chair back and wrapped it around me. The fear increased even more, so I put the blanket over my head.

With my voice trembling, I began rebuking the demon, but the atmosphere of fear increased even more. Suddenly, the demon began to manifest its ferocity by grabbing the chair and tipping it forward, causing me to fall out. I still clutched the blanket, so the demon ripped it from my hands and flung it to the floor. At that point the curtains began flapping as if blown by a strong wind, and then they were ripped off the window. I stood up and surveyed the chaotic mess and realized that the demon was putting on a show, like a display of power.

Suddenly I was filled with crazy boldness and courage, causing all fear to vanish. I jumped to my feet in the realization of who I was in Christ and began wildly dancing throughout the room, singing the name of Jesus over and over. Then I broke out into laughter as I realized that my focus had been on getting rid of the demon, rather than the assignment that it was sent to perform. The assignment was fear and as I overcame fear with the boldness imparted by the Lord. As I began to dance and rejoice the demonic spirit shrieked—now it was the wicked thing that was afraid! —and ran from the house. At that point I woke up.

DANCE ON IT!

Have you been harassed by the enemy? Has he tried to knock you out of your posture of confidence in the Lord, like me being tipped out of my chair? Has he tried to disrupt things around you the same way he yanked the blanket off me and tore the drapes down? If so, it just might be time for you to "dance on it" with great abandon. Remember who you are! You are a child of the King and timidity and fear has no place in you.

The enemy's assignment is to attempt to sow fear. This is what the demon in my dream wanted to maintain in order to continue to occupy the house and control its atmosphere. It targeted the things that I initially went to for safety as I felt the fear within the walls of the room. First, I found comfort in the chair and then I added a blanket to hide underneath. Even though I prayed and rebuked the demon, it knew that I was still afraid because I tried to combat its influence while hiding in the comfort of the chair and cowering under the "safety" of the blanket. My confidence in the Lord had succumbed to fear that had targeted my soul. My initial boldness was swallowed up by terrified timidity.

Yet, when those "comforts" were removed, instead of being terrified, the Lord came to my rescue and I was able to stand in His strength and see the absurdity of the wild display that the demon was putting on. I immediately wanted to break out laughing at how afraid I had been and how ridiculous this "show" had been. As the fear left, I just couldn't help myself—I began dancing on the curtains and the blanket that lay strewn on the floor. I jumped and spun and sang, completely free of all fear. The demon that fed on fear had to leave because there was no more fear to empower it.

THE TRUTH WILL SET YOU FREE

The enemy cannot stand it when we stop being afraid of him. This demon had no idea what to do when I arose and began to dance amid its trickery and bluster; it was all too much for it to tolerate. Fear was the assignment and when I overcame fear, the demon had to leave.

We spend too much time rebuking the enemy instead of discerning assignments of evil and dancing upon them with declarations of truth. The truth is that no weapon formed against us will prosper! If the enemy's weapon is fear then it will not prosper, so shed false comforts, put on the powerful shoes of truth, and begin to dance. As truth is released, boldness will follow, and assignments go where they belong: UNDER YOUR FEET!

I love the passages in Isaiah 54:11-17 in The Message translation of the Bible:

> *Afflicted city, storm-battered, unpitied: I'm about to rebuild you with stones of turquoise, lay your foundations with sapphires, construct your towers with rubies, your gates with jewels, and all your walls with precious stones. All your children will have God for their teacher—what a mentor for your chil-*

dren! You'll be built solid, grounded in righteousness, far from any trouble—nothing to fear! Far from terror—it won't even come close!

If anyone attacks you, don't for a moment suppose that I sent them, and if any should attack, nothing will come of it. I create the blacksmith who fires up his forge and makes a weapon designed to kill. I also create the destroyer—but no weapon that can hurt you has ever been forged. Any accuser who takes you to court will be dismissed as a liar. This is what God's servants can expect. I'll see to it that everything works out for the best."

With him is only the arm of flesh, but with us is the Lord our God to help us and to fight our battles." And the people gained confidence from what Hezekiah the king of Judah said. (2 Chronicles 32:8)

Day 26 Declaration

O Israel, rejoice in your Maker. O people of Jerusalem, exult in your King. Praise his name with dancing, accompanied by tambourine and harp. For the Lord delights in his people; he crowns the humble with victory. (Psalm 149:2-4)

I decree that it is time for my soul to receive confident boldness that is found in the Lord. I will not allow the enemy, who choreographs a "dance of fear," to cause me to shrink back or hide in dread. I will no longer hide in comforts that provide no true protection. I will now get up and dance! I will dance upon every bad report, upon every fear, upon injustice, upon everything that has disrupted my life and robbed me of joy and gladness! The Lord crowns me with victory as I put my trust in Him.

27

Great Are You Lord

Rare is the time that I am not filled with courage and boldness when I am spending time exalting the Lord! Singing praises to His name and declaring His nature releases an infusion of confident assurance and fearlessness that connects me intimately to who He is. Worship lifts me from the earthly realm, with all its cares and problems and turmoil that come to weigh me down, and carries me to the heavenly realm where I am lifted above it all.

For he raised us from the dead along with Christ and seated us with him in the heavenly realms because we are united with Christ Jesus. (Ephesians 2:6)

We are seated in heavenly places, united with Christ! We are united to the greatness of the Lord and His greatness moves through us. The God who created the heavens and the earth, who put the stars in the sky and holds all things together, has united us to Him. Worship ushers us into that reality and experience. His power and goodness never leave us or forsake us but worship causes our souls to remember and experience them, joining ourselves to heavenly truth, and from there we declare, "Great are you Lord!"

Often we forget the unfathomable greatness of our God through the hours of each day while we are busy with the mundane tasks of life. Each day we go out into the world more aware of our weaknesses than of His surpassing greatness.

There is not a single day, not a single second, that we are not united to the one who sits upon the throne of grace. All power, all honor, all majesty, all authority, and every created thing that is in heaven and earth belong to Him.

> *Jesus came and told his disciples, "I have been given all authority in heaven and on earth..." (Matthew 28:18)*

Yet, this God who holds all creation in His hands and to whom all authority belongs also cares about every detail of our lives. It is beyond comprehension to imagine this truth. How can His love span such vast horizons and still reach down to personally connect with every detail of our individual lives? It leaves me undone to realize that He values me so greatly. It causes me to boast in Him, "Great are you Lord!" Trying to understand this kind of love is beyond anything our greatest flights of imagination can fathom. Our understanding of human love cannot touch this kind of greatness.

It is amazing and astonishing that we are intimately united to this King of Glory. How is it, then, that we still tremble at the storms of life? How is it that we doubt or question if He sees us or knows our needs? This God who holds all things together also holds our lives His hands. How can we not stand in awe in the face of such love and kindness? Not only does He have authority but through our union with Him we too have authority. We have His Spirit living in us! This is the very power that raised Jesus from the dead, and we are united to that incomprehensible power of His Spirit as well.

That is why we shout, "Great are you, Lord!" Being united to His greatness makes us brave, bold, courageous, and strong.

Day 27 Declaration

'Not by might nor by power, but by my Spirit,' says the LORD Almighty. (Zechariah 4:6)

Today I declare over my life and from the depths of my heart, "Great are you, Lord!" I am seated in heavenly places and united to you each and every day. That does not change! You are enthroned upon my praises therefore I begin and end each day with praise. I remind my soul that the God who holds all things in heaven and earth together is also holding me. He hears my cry before I speak, and He sees my need before I ask. My life is united to Him and His Spirit lives within me. I do not go forth in my might or power but by His Spirit. I will be confident and bold in my life because I am united to Christ.

28

In My Weakness You Are Strong

We have journeyed far on the path of boldness through the power of the Lord. But still, there are days where we just feel weak! We have days that cause us to feel lethargic, helpless, and vulnerable. Other days, we feel strong and confident; energy seems to course through our being, causing us to face the day with the boldness of a lion.

Feelings are powerful tools for both good and evil, for encouragement and discouragement; therefore, we want to be sure to submit our feelings to God's Word so that our lives are aligned with truth rather than ever-changing feelings with their ups and downs, highs and lows.

In January 2016 I was in a serious car accident that in a moment took me from a place of strength to experiencing tremendous physical and emotional weakness. The physical pain was so great that I could not sleep for more than thirty minutes at a time, and during the day I was concentrating on pain management constantly. Apart from a miraculous physical healing, I was forced to deal with my "new norm"; which was weakness. Because I had a household to run—I am a wife, mom, and grandma—and I continued doing ministry, this required me to truly embrace the truth found in 2 Corinthians 12:9,

Each time he said, "My grace is all you need. My power works best in weakness." So now I am glad to boast about my weaknesses, so that the power of Christ can work through me.

I could not rely upon physical or even emotional strength; therefore I had to go to the place of grace that released the power of Christ to work through me. Though my body was weak I was becoming spiritually stronger than ever before, because I had to rely fully upon His grace and His strength working in and through me. We often don't realize how much we lean upon our human strength and our emotional equilibrium to hold us steady until they are removed. When that happens, we quickly realize what we depend on for our source of strength.

While we were raising our children, we also adopted and fostered special-needs children. These individuals had what the world would call "weaknesses": neurological weaknesses, emotional weaknesses, and sometimes physical weaknesses. One of our kids struggled with numerous physical, emotional, and neurological challenges. These "weaknesses" consumed his days with their demands that he had no control over. And yet, this young man pressed into the grace of Christ that caused him to excel in school and go on to graduate from university with his Bachelor of Arts degree. All the while, his weakness was unrelenting, but God's strength was just as unrelenting, giving him the grace to overcome.

We can choose to make our weakness an excuse for failing, becoming a victim, especially when we face challenges that we have no control over. Or, we can be like so many of the heroes in the Bible and boast in our weakness so that the power of Christ can work through us.

I am dyslexic and struggle to read, and yet God has taken that weakness and turned me into a writer. One of our dearest friends is also dyslexic and yet when the Spirit of the Lord falls upon him, he is one of the most dynamic and anointed preachers that I've ever heard. Though these aren't extreme, life-altering weaknesses, they surely pose a struggle for those of us with a public ministry. Most of us who grew up with dyslexia felt as though they were not smart because so much of our schooling involved reading. Yet, as we embraced our weaknesses and learned to depend on God's strength, we found that no weakness is too big for the power of Christ at work in us.

I have learned to be bold and courageous despite my weaknesses because my confidence is in His strength. You too can change the way you look at your weaknesses and allow them to be the very avenue that makes room for the strength and power of Jesus.

DAY 28 DECLARATION

He gives strength to the weary and increases the power of the weak. (Isaiah 40:29)

Today I choose to declare this truth, "In my weakness you give me strength!" Though my weaknesses have caused me to feel insecure and fearful, I willingly put my trust and confidence in you alone. I will not hide or mask my weaknesses but rather I will make them a doorway for your strength to be made manifest in my life. I will not be defined by my weaknesses or allow them to be my identity, for I know that with you I can do all things through Christ who strengthens me.

29

God's Fire on Your Offering

On the top of Mount Carmel, Elijah and the prophets of Baal had an epic showdown. The story is recounted in 1 Kings 18, and as I have been writing this book, the Holy Spirit keeps drawing my attention to their confrontation.

As you recall, Jezebel had been killing the prophets of God and supporting the prophets of Baal and Asherah. When Elijah showed up to meet with King Ahab, Ahab accused him of making trouble in Israel, but Elijah responded,

> *"I have not made trouble for Israel...But you and your father's family have. You have abandoned the Lord's commands and have followed the Baals." (1 Kings 18:18)*

Elijah then told Ahab to order the prophets of Baal and Asherah to be gathered, along with the worshippers of those idols. There were 450 prophets of Baal and 400 prophets of Asherah and one prophet of the true God. Elijah instructed the prophets of the false gods to build an altar of wood, place a cut-up bull on it, and then call to their gods, asking them to send fire to consume the offering. From morning to evening they called, screamed, leaped about, and ritualistically cut themselves to summon their god. Fire never fell.

Then Elijah built an altar of stone and wood. He too placed a cut-up bull upon it. Then the altar was drenched with water; even a trench was dug and filled with water. Then he called upon the one true God.

> *At the usual time for offering the evening sacrifice, Elijah the prophet walked up to the altar and prayed, "O LORD, God of Abraham, Isaac, and Jacob, prove today that you are God in Israel and that I am your servant. Prove that I have done all this at your command. O LORD, answer me! Answer me so these people will know that you, O LORD, are God and that you have brought them back to yourself." Immediately the fire of the LORD flashed down from heaven and burned up the young bull, the wood, the stones, and the dust. It even licked up all the water in the trench! And when all the people saw it, they fell face down on the ground and cried out, "The LORD —he is God! Yes, the LORD is God!" (1 Kings 18:36-39)*

Many of you are facing impossible circumstances and yet you have not turned away from the one true God. You have seen the lives of prophets taken, you have watched the evil one try to kill the word of the Lord that you have been standing on, and you have watched your countrymen turn to serve idols and false gods.

Today you stand like Elijah before your drenched offering, knowing that the God of Abraham, Isaac, and Jacob is the true God. Those against you outnumber those who are for you, but God is on your side and He is about to send fire upon your offering!

I hear you praying the words of Elijah,

> *"...Prove that I have done all this at your command. O LORD, answer me! Answer me so these people will know that you, O LORD, are God and that you have brought them back to yourself."*

This showdown is not merely for your breakthrough, but it is the kindness of God that brings those who have turned to false gods back to the one who loves them and gave His life for them. It is for you, for God, and for those who have been lost.

The spirit of Elijah is upon the church and we are about to see the fire of God fall upon impossibilities and be unleashed on the nations. Many will turn to God as they see Him prove that He alone is God.

Declare that the spirit of Elijah will fall in greater measure upon our sacrifice. Believe that God's true and pure fire will fall. Declare that those who worship and serve idols will turn back to God. The spirit of Elijah defeats every spirit of deception when God's fire falls and reveals Him as the one true God.

This is the hour that the glory will return! The glory train is arriving and a shout of "All aboard" is heard throughout the nations. Those who carry the spirit of Elijah will board this train and be carriers of His fire and glory. They will call back that which belongs to God! The whistle has sounded, and it is the time of glory and fire to go forth with light and power.

We call upon the name of the God of Abraham, Isaac, and Jacob! Prove that we have done all these things at your command. O LORD, answer us. Answer us so the people will know that you, O LORD, are God and that you have brought them back to yourself.

Day 29 Declaration

I have heard all about you, LORD. I am filled with awe by your amazing works. In this time of our deep need, help us again as you did in years gone by. And in your anger, remember your mercy. (Habakkuk 3:2)

I declare this day that you alone are God! I choose to leave everything that has exulted itself against you and I renounce every belief that stands as a contradiction against your Word, your character and your ways. I cry out, "Prove in our day that you alone are God!" Your ways fill me with awe and give me boldness to follow you and declare to the nations who you are. Your love makes me courageous to stand in the midst of my enemies and declare, "Jesus Christ is Lord of all!" Your people are in a time of deep need for our adversaries have risen up in accusations against your ways and your truths. Remember mercy in the midst of the nation's that have turned away from you. Remember mercy and help us, Lord!

30

The Lion of Judah

I end our journey together by telling you about a powerful encounter I had as I was writing this book. The Holy Spirit took me into an amazing visionary experience. It suddenly and supernaturally filled me with new boldness and courage that I had not experienced before. I know that this is not meant for a limited few, but is a word for the people of God. I pray that it will give you courage to step out in new boldness.

I was taken to a land where I saw a small lamb walking toward a walled and fortified city. I somehow knew that this tiny lamb was going out to see the walls of this city fall. The enemy's troops that stood on the walls of the city saw the lamb approaching and began to sneer and bellow with mocking laughter as it came near. Then I became the lamb and noticed that as I moved, there were what appeared to be four posts with a canopy that moved over me as I walked. My first thought was that it was a "moving chuppah"— the four-poled canopy a Jewish couple stands under during their wedding ceremony.

As I walked toward the fortified city, I understood that I was to open my mouth and shout, even though I knew it would merely come out as a small bleat of "baa." I drew a breath but as I opened my mouth to shout, I heard a mighty roar! This roar was so loud that the walls of the city fell, crushing the enemy soldiers that mocked me. I somehow knew that this "covering" was the thing that defeated the enemy and made the walls fall.

The scene changed and I once again saw the lamb who was like young David, approaching the giant Goliath. I saw the four posts and the canopy moving over this lamb once again. Then suddenly my eyes were opened to see that what I thought was a chuppah was actually the Lion of Judah. The four posts were His four legs and the white sheet or canopy was His belly. As the little lamb moved, the Lion of Judah moved and covered it wherever it went.

Once again, the lamb knew to release a shout at this giant, and when it opened its mouth to bleat, the same mighty roar thundered over the plain and slew the giant with its power. When the lamb released its small sound, the Lion released His mighty power. The lamb's bold courage came from the One who moved with it and covered it with protection and power.

As I came out of this experience I was immediately filled with a new courage! I knew that this was a picture of our constant spiritual reality. The Lion of Judah moves with each one of His lambs. We can face fortified walls, enemy armies, and giants with bold confidence because our obedience is partnered with the full power of our King, the Commander of the hosts of heaven. What sounds like a small, frail bleat to us becomes the mighty roar of the Lion, the sound of many waters, the voice of the LORD that strips the cedars bare. Where we go, He goes.

The Lion of Judah is your canopy, adding His roar to your small sound and releasing His might and power to your acts of obedience. He is your bold confidence! Go forward in His strength, His leading, His anointing, and walk in the boldness provided for you by the mighty one who protects you and loves you.

Through you, He is expanding His kingdom of truth and righteousness. So be bold and courageous!

A shoot will come up from the stump of Jesse;
 from his roots a Branch will bear fruit.
The Spirit of the Lord will rest on him—
 the Spirit of wisdom and of understanding,
 the Spirit of counsel and of might,
 the Spirit of the knowledge and fear of the Lord—
and he will delight in the fear of the Lord.

He will not judge by what he sees with his eyes,
 or decide by what he hears with his ears;
but with righteousness he will judge the needy,
 with justice he will give decisions for the poor of the earth.
He will strike the earth with the rod of his mouth;
 with the breath of his lips he will slay the wicked.
Righteousness will be his belt
 and faithfulness the sash around his waist.

The wolf will live with the lamb,
 the leopard will lie down with the goat,
the calf and the lion and the yearling together;
 and a little child will lead them.
The cow will feed with the bear,
 their young will lie down together,
 and the lion will eat straw like the ox.
The infant will play near the cobra's den,
 and the young child will put its hand into the viper's nest.
They will neither harm nor destroy
 on all my holy mountain,
for the earth will be filled with the knowledge of the Lord
 as the waters cover the sea. (Isaiah 11:1-9)

Day 30 Declaration

Today is the first day of the rest of my life. Though I am but a small lamb, I go out under the covering of the Lion of Judah. My quiet "baa" is met with His resounding roar, my gentle steps are partnered with His tread that shakes the nations, my obedience is powered by His righteousness and justice, my fight is made complete by His victory. I go forth in the fear of the Lord, who is the Lion of Judah. I go forth in bold confidence in who He is and how He goes with me. It is time for the Lion and the lamb to move as one!

Sources

Page 3 Eisenhower, William D. "Fearing God" quoted in *Christianity Today,* accessed December 11, 2018, https://www.christianitytoday.com/biblestudies/bible-answers/spirituallife/what-does-it-mean-to-fear-god.html

Page 43 "St. Patrick's Breastplate" is an ancient prayer attributed to Patrick of Ireland. It was translated as the hymn "I Bind Unto Myself Today" by Cecil Frances Alexander (April 1818 – October 1895)